Six Days

How long were the days in Genesis 1?

ARE SIX LITERAL DAYS NECESSARY? • DID JESUS SAY HE CREATED IN SIX DAYS? • COULD GOD REALLY HAVE CREATED EVERYTHING IN SIX DAYS? • EISEGESIS: A GENESIS VIRUS • DID BIBLE AUTHORS BELIEVE IN A LITERAL GENESIS? • IS THE AGE OF THE EARTH A SALVATION ISSUE?

A POCKET GUIDE TO . . .

Six Days

How long were the days in Genesis 1?

1:1
answersingenesis
Petersburg, Kentucky, USA

Reprinted September 2014

ISBN: 978-1-60092-994-6

Printed in China.

www.answersingenesis.org

Table of Contents

Introduction

*I*n the church today, we see a number of approaches to the days of creation recorded in Genesis 1. Some say that they were literal, approximately 24-hour days. Others take them to be long periods of time, during which the great epochs of evolutionary history occurred. Others believe that they were 24 hours each, but they also insert a long gap to account for the vast ages of secular geology. And still others treat the entire account as nothing more than poetry, insisting that Genesis has nothing to do with when or how God created the world.

But, which of these views is correct? How can we determine if the six days of creation were actual days or something else? And is it really all that important of an issue?

This *Pocket Guide to Six Days* will answer these questions and more. We'll examine the words of Jesus Himself and explore the views of Paul and other biblical authors. We'll see that what we believe about the length of the creation days affects a host of other issues, such as our view of Scripture and God's character.

Since the Bible is God's inspired, inerrant Word, we can trust it to give us clear information about the past.

The Necessity for Believing in Six Literal Days

Ken Ham

The majority of Christians in churches probably aren't sure whether God really created everything in six literal days. Many believe it doesn't matter whether it took six days or six million years. However, it is vital to believe in six literal days for many reasons. Foremost is that allowing these days to be long periods of time undermines the foundations of the message of the Cross.

Why do people doubt the days?

The major reason why people doubt that the days of creation are 24-hour literal days usually has nothing to do with what the Bible says, but comes from outside influences. For example, many believe that because scientists have supposedly proved the earth to be billions of years old then the days of creation cannot be ordinary days.

If people use Scripture to try to justify that the days of creation are long periods of time, they usually quote passages such as 2 Peter 3:8, ". . . one day is with the Lord as a thousand years . . ." Because of this, they think the days could be a thousand years, or perhaps even millions of years. However, if you look at the rest of the verse, it says, ". . . and a thousand years as one day." This cancels out their argument! The context of this passage concerns the Second Coming of the Lord Jesus Christ. This particular verse is telling people that with God, waiting a day is like waiting a thousand years, and waiting a thousand years is like waiting a day because God is outside of time—He is not limited by natural processes and time. This has absolutely *nothing* to do with defining the days of creation. Besides, the word "day" already exists and has been defined, which is why in

Second Peter it can be compared to a thousand years. There is no reference in this passage to the days of creation.

Some appeal to fossils allegedly being millions of years old. But fossils are the remains of dead creatures and plants buried by water. Many fossils clearly show death consistent with sudden, catastrophic burial, supporting the Bible's account of a worldwide Flood.

What does "day" mean?

The Hebrew word for day in Genesis chapter 1 is the word *yom*. It is important to understand that almost any word can have two or more meanings, depending on context. We need to understand the context of the usage of this word in Genesis chapter 1.[1]

Respected Hebrew dictionaries, like the Brown, Driver, Briggs lexicon, give a number of meanings for the word *yom* depending upon context. One of the passages they give for *yom*'s meaning an ordinary day happens to be Genesis chapter 1. The reason is obvious. Every time the word *yom* is used with a number, or with the phrase "evening and morning', anywhere in the Old Testament, it always means an ordinary day. In Genesis chapter 1, for each of the six days of creation, the Hebrew word *yom* is used with a number *and* the phrase, "evening and morning.' There is no doubt that the writer is being emphatic that these are ordinary days.

Would someone apply this to the empty grave? If we allow our children to doubt the days of creation, when the language speaks so plainly, they are likely to then doubt Christ's Virgin Birth, and that He really rose from the dead.

What if the days were millions of years?

The idea of millions of years came from the belief that the fossil record was built up over a long time. As soon as people allow for millions of years, they allow for the fossil record to be millions of years old. This creates an insurmountable problem regarding the gospel. The fossil record consists of the death of billions of creatures. In fact, it is a record of death, disease, suffering, cruelty, and brutality. It is a very ugly record.

The Bible is adamant though, that death, disease, and suffering came into the world as a result of sin. God instituted death and bloodshed because of sin so man could be redeemed. As soon as Christians allow for death, suffering, and disease before sin, then the whole foundations of the message of the Cross and the Atonement have been destroyed. The doctrine of original sin, then, is totally undermined.

If there were death, disease, and suffering before Adam rebelled—then what did sin do to the world? What does Paul mean in Romans 8 when he says the whole of creation groans in pain because of the Curse? How can all things be restored in the future to no more death and suffering, unless the beginning was also free of death and suffering? The whole message of the gospel falls apart if one allows millions of years for the creation of the world.

The whole of the creation restored . . . to what? The Bible says there will be a future restoration (Acts 3:21), with no death or suffering. How could all things be restored in the future to no more death and suffering unless the beginning was also free of death and suffering? The whole message of the gospel falls apart if you allow millions of years (with death and suffering) for the world's creation.

How should we approach Scripture?

One of the major problems we all have (in fact, it is the same problem Adam and Eve had) is that we tend to start from outside God's Word and then go to what God has written in the Bible (or—in Adam's case—what God said directly to him) to try to interpret it on the basis of our own ideas. This is really the major reason why most people question the days of creation.

We need to realize that the Bible is God's Word. And as it is the inspired Word of the infinite Creator, God, then it must be self-authenticating and self-attesting. Thus, we should always start with what God's Word says regardless of outside ideas. Only God's Word is infallible.

If we allow our children to accept the possibility that we can doubt the days of creation when the language speaks so plainly, then we are teaching them a particular approach to all of Scripture. Why shouldn't they then start to doubt that Christ's Virgin Birth really means a virgin birth? Why shouldn't they start to doubt that the Resurrection really means resurrection?

In fact, there are many theologians who doubt these very things, as they have come to disbelieve the plain words of Scripture written in the foundational Book of Genesis.

The Bible is the correct foundation to look at all other things. If we don't start there then we are starting with the wrong foundation. The Apostle Paul needed to get the Greeks back to the correct foundation when he was preaching. The Paul was grieved when he found the city of Athens steeped in idolatry (Acts 17:16). When he noticed the altar "to the unknown god," he used the opportunity to tell the philosophers that their unknown god is God the Creator, Lord of heaven and earth. Sometimes we need to echo this same sentiment within the church—to get back to God's Word as the foundation from the very first verse.

Why did God take six days?

If you think about it, an infinite Creator God could have created everything in no time. Why, then, did He take as long as six days? The answer is given in Exodus 20:11. Here we find that God tells us that He deliberately took six days and rested for one as a pattern for man—this is where the seven-day week comes from. The seven-day week has no basis for existing except from Scripture. If one believes that the days of creation are long periods of time, then the week becomes meaningless.

The Bible tells us that Adam was created on the sixth day. If he lived through day six and day seven, and then died when he was 930 years old, and if each of these days was a thousand or a million years, you have major problems! On the fourth day of creation (Genesis 1:14–19), we are given the comparison of day to night, and days to years. If the word "day" doesn't mean an ordinary day, then the comparison of day to night and day to years becomes meaningless.

Was there death, pain, and suffering before Adam and Eve's sin? At the close of the Creation Week, God called everything He had made "very good." This is powerful evidence against the idea that long ages of suffering and dying took place before the first man and woman, Adam and Eve, appeared. Were the days 24 hours? Most definitely! "Let God be true, but every man a liar" (Romans 3:4).

---

1.   For discussion on the few uses of *yom* in which the meaning is disputed, see "The Days of Creation: A Semantic Approach," by James Stambaugh, *CEN Tech. J.*, Vol. 5(1), 1991, pp. 70–78.

Ken Ham, President and CEO, Answers in Genesis–USA & the Creation Museum

Ken's bachelor's degree in applied science (with an emphasis on environmental biology) was awarded by the Queensland Institute of Technology in Australia. He also holds a diploma of education from the University of Queensland. In recognition of the contribution Ken has made to the church in the USA and internationally, Ken has been awarded two honorary doctorates: a Doctor of Divinity (1997) from Temple Baptist College in Cincinnati, Ohio and a Doctor of Literature (2004) from Liberty University in Lynchburg, Virginia.

Since moving to America in 1987, Ken has become one of the most in-demand Christian conference speakers and talk show guests in America. He has appeared on national shows such as Fox's *The O'Reilly Factor* and *Fox and Friends in the Morning*; CNN's *The Situation Room with Wolf Blitzer*, ABC's *Good Morning America*, the BBC, *CBS News Sunday Morning*, *The NBC Nightly News with Brian Williams*, and *The PBS News Hour with Jim Lehrer*.

Did Jesus Say He Created in Six Days?

Ken Ham

A rather vehement "old-earther" wrote recently and claimed: "a twenty-four [hour] understanding of the creation days was never stated explicitly by Jesus . . . ." Well, did Jesus anywhere clearly state that the earth was created in six ordinary (approximately 24 hours each) days?

When confronted with such a question, most Christians would automatically go to the New Testament to read the recorded words of Jesus to see if such a statement occurs.

Now, when we search the New Testament Scriptures, we certainly find many interesting statements Jesus made that relate to this issue. For instance:

1. "But from the beginning of the creation 'God made them male and female.'" (Mark 10:6). This makes it clear that Jesus taught the creation was young, for Adam and Eve existed "from the beginning"—not billions of years after the universe and earth came into existence.

2. "Do not think that I shall accuse you to the Father; there is one who accuses you—Moses, in whom you trust. For if you believed Moses, you would believe Me; for he wrote about Me. But if you do not believe his writings, how will you believe My words?" (John 5:45–47). In this passage, Jesus makes it clear that one must believe what Moses wrote. And one of the passages in the writings of Moses in Exodus 20:11 states: "For in six days the LORD made the heavens and the earth, the sea, and all that is in them, and rested the seventh day. Therefore

the LORD blessed the Sabbath day and hallowed it." This, of course, is the basis of our seven-day week—six days work and one day rest. Obviously, this passage was meant to be taken as speaking of a total of seven literal days based on the Creation Week of six literal days of work and one literal day of rest.

In fact, in Luke 13:14, in his response to Jesus healing a person on the Sabbath, the ruler of the synagogue obviously referred to this passage when he said, "There are six days on which men ought to work; therefore come and be healed on them, and not on the Sabbath day." The Sabbath day here was considered an ordinary day, and the six days of work were considered ordinary days. This teaching is based on the law of Moses as recorded in Exodus 20, where we find the Ten Commandments—the six-day Creation Week being a basis for the Fourth Commandment.

One could consider many more passages that certainly imply that Jesus taught that He created in six days, but are there any explicit passages?

I believe there are. However, one has to approach this issue in a slightly different manner. Why just go to the New Testament to try to find out if Jesus stated He created in six days?

Why not the Old Testament? After all, Jesus is the second person of the Godhead, and has always existed.

First, Colossians makes it clear that Jesus Christ, the Son of God, was the one who created all things: "For by Him all things were created that are in heaven, and that are on earth, visible and invisible, whether thrones or dominions or principalities or powers. All things were created through Him and for Him. And He is before all things, and in Him all things consist" (Colossians 1:16–17).

We are also told elsewhere in Scripture how Jesus created: "By the word of the Lord the heavens were made, And all the host of them by the breath of His mouth . . . For He spoke, and it was done" (Psalm 33:6, 33:9).

As well as this, we know that Jesus is in fact called "the Word":

"In the beginning was the Word, and the Word was with God, and the Word was God. He was in the beginning with God. All things were made through Him, and without Him nothing was made that was made." (John 1:1–3).

So Jesus, who is the Word, created by speaking everything into existence.

Now, consider Exodus 20:1: "And God spoke all these words, saying . . . ." Because Jesus is the Word, this must be a reference to the preincarnate Christ speaking to Moses. As we know, there are a number of appearances of Christ ("theophanies") in the Old Testament.

John 1:18 states: "No one has seen God at any time. The only begotten Son, who is in the bosom of the Father, He has declared Him." There is no doubt, with rare exception, that the pre-incarnate Christ did the speaking to Adam, Noah, the patriarchs, Moses, etc.

Now, when the Creator God spoke as recorded in Exodus 20, what did He (Jesus) say? As we read on, we find this statement: "For in six days the LORD made the heavens and the earth, the sea, and all that is in them, and rested the seventh day . . ."

Yes, Jesus did explicitly say He created in six days.[1] Not only this, but the one who spoke the words "six days" also wrote them down for Moses: "Then the LORD delivered to me two tablets of stone written with the finger of God, and on them were all the words which the LORD had spoken to you on the mountain from the midst of the fire in the day of the assembly" (Deuteronomy 9:10).

Jesus said clearly: He created in six days! And He even did something He didn't do with most of Scripture—He wrote it down Himself. How more authoritative can you get than that?

---

1.   Even if someone is convinced that God the Father was the speaker in Exodus 20:11, the Father and Son would never disagree. Jesus said in John 10:30: "I and My Father are one" [neuter—one in the essence of deity, not one in personality].

24 Hours—Plain as Day

Jud Davis

In 1983, as a Junior, I walked into the University of Georgia's religion building terrified. The professor was an expert in Hebrew from Yale University. I had been a Christian for only two years, and I wanted to learn that language.

I knew that the religion department doubted the authorship of Old Testament books. For them, the myth *Enuma Elish* was more important for understanding Genesis than was Moses, Paul, or Jesus. Most of them believed that evolution disproved Christianity once and for all. Jesus was just a man, and the Bible was a book like any other book—written only by man and full of errors.

I knew at the core of this secular approach to Bible study was the axiom that human reason is supreme. They believed that scholars are over, rather than under, God's Word. So I anxiously wondered how studying Hebrew in a secular setting might help or hurt my faith.

The Bible, however, has an intrinsic, self-authenticating power—a power even skeptics cannot destroy. In spite of skeptical attacks, the Hebrew language has remained a passion of my life for almost thirty years. I focused my doctoral work in England on the New Testament use of the Old Testament, and my continuous study of Hebrew since then has reaffirmed the supernatural nature of God's Word and its truth at every point.

I teach at a Christian college that hosts a conference every year on a contemporary hot topic. Last year the school decided to host one on the proper reading of Genesis 1–2. The goal was to gather all the major evangelical scholars for a two-day conference and let them present their cases for different ways to read the first two chapters of Genesis.

The school stumbled on a serious problem—we could not find a nationally recognized Old Testament scholar who held the traditional view that the world was created in six, 24-hour days.

During my search, I even went to the national Evangelical Theological Society (ETS) meeting and attended the session on Genesis 1–2. During a panel discussion, some scholars began to openly mock the traditional view. Others assured the audience that *Enuma Elish*, and the like, were the key to understanding Genesis. I felt like I was back in Peabody Hall. What was happening?

When I left ETS, I was confused. Did the majority of evangelical scholars really believe that the Hebrew text failed to support the traditional view? Did they believe that no one who studies Hebrew seriously believes that God supernaturally created everything in six days a few thousand years ago?

Time for investigation

This experience bothered me so badly that I started doing more research. I knew that modern critical scholars think the day-age view and the more recent framework hypothesis are grammatically untenable from the standpoint of the original author's intent. One of the best Hebraists in the world, James Barr of Oxford University, had written in a letter twenty years ago, "So far as I know, there is no professor of Hebrew or Old Testament at any world-class university who does not believe that the writer(s) of Gen. 1–11 intended to convey to their readers the ideas that (a) creation took place in a series of six days which were the same as the days of 24 hours we now experience (b) the figures contained in the Genesis genealogies provided by simple addition a chronology from the beginning of the world up to later stages in the biblical story."[1]

I wondered what modern "world-class" Hebraists would say about Barr's statement today, so I tracked down several leading experts to ask their opinion.

Hugh Williamson is the current Regius Professor of Hebrew at Oxford University. Oxford is perhaps the most prestigious university in the world, and Williamson is one of the top Hebraists anywhere. In an email he responded, "So far as the days of Genesis 1 are concerned, I am sure that Professor Barr was correct. . . . I have not met any Hebrew professors who had the slightest doubt about this unless they were already committed to some alternative by other considerations that do not arise from a straightforward reading of the Hebrew text as it stands."[2]

I also emailed Barr's letter to Emanuel Tov of Hebrew University Jerusalem; he would be on anyone's list of Hebrew experts. Professor Tov responded in kind: "For the biblical people this was history, difficult as it is for us to accept this view."[3] Here was confirmation from a Jewish man who spoke and thought in Hebrew.

There is a residential theological research library called Tyndale House, located outside of Cambridge University in England. You can rent a room and literally live in the library. It is perhaps the best such facility in the world. During its history some of the top scholars have been its "warden." The current warden is a young man of encyclopedic knowledge named Peter Williams. He sent a paper to me that said, "Although the Young Universe Creationist position is not widely held within secular academia, the position—that the author of Genesis 1 maintained that the world was created in six literal days—is nearly universally held."[4]

I could go on, listing dozens and dozens of names, but there is no need. The scholarship is clear. The writer of Genesis 1–2 meant the text to teach chronology in terms of normal days. So why would almost the entirety of evangelical scholarship reject the author's intent?

When a day is not a day

My inability to find many evangelical scholars who support the traditional view was puzzling for another reason: evangelicals' public commitment to the inerrancy of Scripture. The Chicago Statement on Biblical Inerrancy, signed in 1978, gives the fullest statement on what evangelicals believe about the Bible. Article 12 says of creation and the Flood, "We deny that Biblical infallibility and inerrancy are limited to spiritual, religious, or redemptive themes, exclusive of assertions in the fields of history and science. We further deny that scientific hypotheses about earth history may properly be used to overturn the teaching of Scripture on creation and the flood."

I was confused why many of the signers did not believe in the traditional view of Genesis 1–2. So I started emailing people I knew who had signed the document. What I found out was shocking. Henry Morris had proposed the language for Article 12, and he meant it to exclude long ages and theistic evolution.[5] Many of the signers decided to reject Morris's intended meaning and reinterpret his words in line with their own beliefs.

This was the same thing that happened among Bible-believing churches at the turn of the twentieth century, during the early rise of modernist theology. Ministers in the Presbyterian Church, for example, would affirm the Westminster Confession, but they would self-interpret the words. So where the confession said that Jesus is God, the liberal minister agreed but meant that Jesus had a God-consciousness like any other man.

This is theological doublespeak. I am surprised that evangelicals are stumbling down the same dead-end path that wrecked mainline churches a century ago.

Days ahead

I would ask my evangelical brothers some basic questions. If the text of Genesis 1–2 does not mean to teach traditional chronology and 24-hour days,[6]

1. Why does Jesus take Genesis 1–2 as teaching history (Matthew 19:4; Mark 10:6)?

2. Why does Paul take it as history (Romans 5:12; 1 Corinthians

11:8–9, 15:21–22, 15:45; 1 Timothy 2:12–14)?

3. Why do nearly all world-class Hebraists assume that the writer of Genesis intended normal days and the text as history?

4. Why did the ancient, medieval, and modern church—until about 1800—have few commentators (if any) who believed in an ancient universe?

5. Why do all of the ancient translations and paraphrases, such as the Aramaic Targums, take the words at face value and translate them as "days," with no hint that they might mean "ages" in Genesis 1?

6. Why is there little or no classical Rabbinic support for an ancient universe?

7. Why are there well-qualified PhD scientists who still support physical data as consistent with a young-earth view?

Nobody has provided me with answers that point to anything but a traditional view of the original meaning. Anyone who says that a closer study of the Hebrew leads elsewhere is simply incorrect. The original intent is plain—a day was a day, from the very first miraculous day.

---

1. Note that Barr does not believe in inerrancy; he is simply affirming the authorial intent of Genesis 1–2.

2. Email to the author, January 7, 2011.

3. Email to the author, December 28, 2010.

4. "No Agony Before Adam," paper given at University of Aberdeen, December 17, 2008, p. 1.

5. In a telephone conversation, one of the coauthors of *The Genesis Flood*, Dr. John Whitcomb, told me that Dr. Henry Morris, the other coauthor of that foundational book in modern creationism, was the proposer of the language. Both were signers of the Chicago Statement.

6. See Terry Mortenson, "Jesus, Evangelical Scholars, and the Age of the Earth," *The Master's Seminary Journal* 18 (2007): 69–98, reprinted at www.answersingenesis.org.

Jud Davis is Professor of Greek and Chair of the Christian Studies and Philosophy Division at Bryan College.

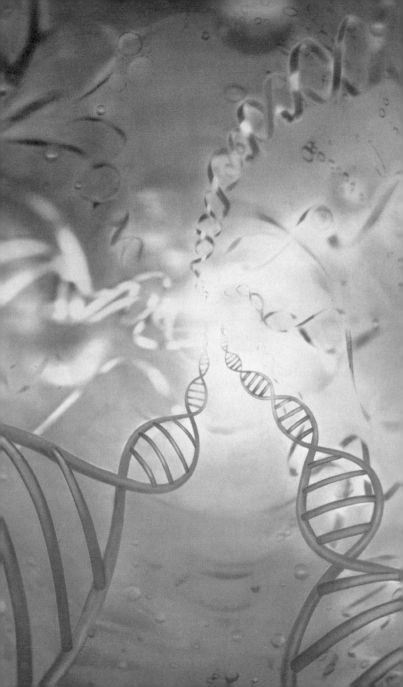

Could God Really Have Created Everything in Six Days?

Ken Ham

Why is it important?

If the days of creation are really geologic ages of millions of years, then the gospel message is undermined at its foundation because it puts death, disease, thorns, and suffering *before* the Fall. The effort to define "days" as "geologic ages" results from an erroneous approach to Scripture—reinterpreting the Word of God on the basis of the fallible theories of sinful people.

It is a good exercise to read Genesis 1 and try to put aside outside influences that may cause you to have a predetermined idea of what the word "day" may mean. Just let the words of the passage speak to you.

Taking Genesis 1 in this way, at face value, without doubt it says that God created the universe, the earth, the sun, moon and stars, plants and animals, and the first two people within six ordinary (approximately 24-hour) days. Being really honest, you would have to admit that you could never get the idea of millions of years from reading this passage.

The majority of Christians (including many Christian leaders) in the Western world, however, do not insist that these days of creation were ordinary-length days, and many of them accept and teach, based on outside influences, that they must have been long periods of time—even millions or billions of years.

How does God communicate to us?

God communicates through language. When He made the first man, Adam, He had already "programmed" him with a language, so there could be communication. Human language consists of words used in a specific context that relates to the entire reality around us.

Thus, God can reveal things to man, and man can communicate with God, because words have meaning and convey an understandable message. If this were not so, how could any of us communicate with each other or with God?

Why "long days"?

Romans 3:4 declares: "Let God be true, and every man a liar." In *every* instance where someone has *not* accepted the "days" of creation to be ordinary days, they have not allowed the words of Scripture to speak to them in context, as the language requires for communication. They have been influenced by ideas from *outside* of Scripture. Thus, they have set a precedent that could allow any word to be reinterpreted by the preconceived ideas of the person reading the words. Ultimately, this will lead to a communication breakdown, as the same words in the same context could mean different things to different people.

The church fathers

Most church fathers accepted the days of creation as ordinary days.[1] It is true that some of the early church fathers did not teach the days of creation as ordinary days—but many of them had been influenced by Greek philosophy, which caused them to interpret the days as allegorical. They reasoned that the creation days were related to God's activities, and God being timeless meant that the days could not be related to human time.[2] In contrast to today's allegorizers, they could not accept that God took *as long as* six days.

Thus, the non-literal days resulted from extra biblical influences (i.e., influences from *outside* the Bible), not from the words of the Bible.

This approach has affected the way people interpret Scripture to this day. As the man who started the Reformation said,

> The days of creation were ordinary days in length. We must understand that these days were actual days (*veros dies*), contrary to the opinion of the Holy Fathers. Whenever we observe that the opinions of the Fathers disagree with Scripture, we reverently bear with them and acknowledge them to be our elders. Nevertheless, we do not depart from the authority of Scripture for their sake.[3]

Again and again, such leaders admit that Genesis 1, taken in a straightforward way, seems to teach six ordinary days. But they then say that this cannot be because of the age of the universe or some other extra biblical reason.

Consider the following representative quotes from Bible scholars who are considered to be conservative yet who do not accept the days of creation as ordinary-length days:

From a superficial reading of Genesis 1, the impression would seem to be that the entire creative process took place in six twenty-four-hour days. . . . This seems to run counter to modern scientific research, which indicates that the planet earth was created several billion years ago.[4]

We have shown the possibility of God's having formed the earth and its life in a series of creative days representing long periods. In view of the apparent age of the earth, this is not only possible—it is probable.[5]

It is as if these theologians view "nature" as a "67th book of the Bible," albeit with more authority than the 66 written books. Rather, we should consider the words of Charles Haddon Spurgeon, the renowned "prince of preachers," in 1877:

We are invited, brethren, most earnestly to go away from the old-fashioned belief of our forefathers because of the supposed discoveries of science. What is science? The method by which man tries to conceal his ignorance. It should not be so, but so it is. You are not to be dogmatical in theology, my brethren, it is wicked; but for scientific men it is the correct thing. You are never to assert anything very strongly; but scientists may boldly assert what they cannot prove, and may demand a faith far more credulous than any we possess. Forsooth, you and I are to take our Bibles and shape and mould our belief according to the evershifting teachings of so-called scientific men. What folly is this! Why, the march of science, falsely so called, through the world may be traced by exploded fallacies and abandoned theories. Former explorers once adored are now ridiculed; the continual wreckings of false hypotheses is a matter of universal notoriety. You may tell where the learned have encamped by the debris left behind of suppositions and theories as plentiful as broken bottles.[6]

Those who would use historical science (as propounded by

people who, by and large, ignore God's written revelation) to interpret the Bible, to teach us things about God, have matters front to back. Because we are fallen, fallible creatures, we need God's written Word, illuminated by the Holy Spirit, to properly understand natural history. The respected systematic theologian Berkhof said:

> Since the entrance of sin into the world, man can gather true knowledge about God from His general revelation only if he studies it in the light of Scripture, in which the elements of God's original self-revelation, which were obscured and perverted by the blight of sin, are republished, corrected, and interpreted. . . . Some are inclined to speak of God's general revelation as a second source; but this is hardly correct in view of the fact that nature can come into consideration here only as interpreted in the light of Scripture.[7]

In other words, Christians should build their thinking on the Bible, not on science.

The "days" of Genesis 1

What does the Bible tell us about the meaning of "day" in Genesis 1? A word can have more than one meaning, depending on the context. For instance, the English word "day" can have perhaps 14 different meanings. For example, consider the following sentence: "Back in my grandfather's day, it took 12 days to drive across the country during the day."

Here the first occurrence of "day" means "time" in a general sense. The second "day," where a number is used, refers to an ordinary day, and the third refers to the daylight portion of the 24-hour period. The point is that words can have more than one meaning, depending on the context.

To understand the meaning of "day" in Genesis 1, we need to determine how the Hebrew word for "day," *yom*, is used in the context of Scripture. Consider the following:

1. A typical concordance will illustrate that *yom* can have a range of meanings: a period of light as contrasted to night, a 24-hour period, time, a specific point of time, or a year.

2. A classic, well-respected Hebrew-English lexicon[8] (a dictionary) has seven headings and many subheadings for the meaning of *yom*—but it defines the creation days of Genesis 1 as ordinary days under the heading "day as defined by evening and morning."

3. A number and the phrase "evening and morning" are used with each of the six days of creation (Genesis 1:5, 1:8, 1:13, 1:19, 1:23, 1:31).

4. Outside Genesis 1, yom is used with a number 359 times, and each time it means an ordinary day.[9] Why would Genesis 1 be the exception?[10]

5. Outside Genesis 1, *yom* is used with the word "evening" or "morning"[11] 23 times. "Evening" and "morning" appear in association, but without *yom*, 38 times. All 61 times the text refers to an ordinary day. Why would Genesis 1 be the exception?[12]

6. In Genesis 1:5, *yom* occurs in context with the word "night." Outside of Genesis 1, "night" is used with *yom* 53 times, and each time it means an ordinary day. Why would Genesis 1 be the exception? Even the usage of the word "light" with *yom* in this passage determines the meaning as ordinary day.[13]

7. The plural of *yom*, which does not appear in Genesis 1, can be used to communicate a longer time period, such as "in those days."[14] Adding a number here would be nonsensical. Clearly, in Exodus 20:11, where a number is used with "days," it unambiguously refers to six earth-rotation days.

8. There are words in biblical Hebrew (such as *olam* or *qedem*)

that are very suitable for communicating long periods of time, or indefinite time, but *none* of these words are used in Genesis 1.[15] Alternatively, the days or years could have been compared with grains of sand if long periods were meant.

Dr. James Barr (Regius Professor of Hebrew at Oxford University), who himself does not believe Genesis is true history, nonetheless admitted as far as the language of Genesis 1 is concerned that

> So far as I know, there is no professor of Hebrew or Old Testament at any world-class university who does not believe that the writer(s) of Gen. 1–11 intended to convey to their readers the ideas that (a) creation took place in a series of six days which were the same as the days of 24 hours we now experience (b) the figures contained in the Genesis genealogies provided by simple addition a chronology from the beginning of the world up to later stages in the biblical story (c) Noah's Flood was understood to be worldwide and extinguish all human and animal life except for those in the ark.[16]

In like manner, nineteenth century liberal Professor Marcus Dods, New College, Edinburgh, said,

> If, for example, the word "day" in these chapters does not mean a period of twenty-four hours, the interpretation of Scripture is hopeless.[17]

Conclusion about "day" in Genesis 1

If we are prepared to let the words of the language speak to us in accord with the context and normal definitions, without being influenced by outside ideas, then the word for "day" found in Genesis 1—which is qualified by a number, the phrase "evening and morning" and for Day 1 the words "light and darkness"—*obviously* means an ordinary day (about 24 hours).

In Martin Luther's day, some of the church fathers were saying that God created everything in only one day or in an instant. Martin Luther wrote,

> When Moses writes that God created Heaven and Earth and whatever is in them in six days, then let this period continue to have been six days, and do not venture to devise any comment according to which six days were one day. But, if you cannot understand how this could have been done in six days, then grant the Holy Spirit the honor of being more learned than you are. For you are to deal with Scripture in such a way that you bear in mind that God Himself says what is written. But since God is speaking, it is not fitting for you wantonly to turn His Word in the direction you wish to go.[18]

Similarly, John Calvin stated, "Albeit the duration of the world, now declining to its ultimate end, has not yet attained six thousand years. . . . God's work was completed not in a moment but in six days."[19]

Luther and Calvin were the backbone of the Protestant Reformation that called the church back to Scripture—*Sola Scriptura* (Scripture alone). Both of these men were adamant that Genesis 1 taught six ordinary days of creation—only thousands of years ago.

Why six days?

Exodus 31:12 says that God commanded Moses to say to the children of Israel:

> Six days may work be done, but on the seventh is the sabbath of rest, holy to the Lord. Whoever does any work in the Sabbath day, he shall surely be put to death. Therefore the sons of Israel shall keep the Sabbath, to observe the Sabbath throughout their generations, for an everlasting covenant. It is a sign between me and the sons of Israel forever.

> For in six days the Lord made the heavens and the earth, and on the seventh day He rested, and was refreshed (Exodus 31:15–17).

Then God gave Moses two tablets of stone upon which were written the commandments of God, written by the finger of God (Exodus 31:18).

Because God is infinite in power and wisdom, there's no doubt He could have created the universe and its contents in no time at all, or six seconds, or six minutes, or six hours—after all, with God nothing shall be impossible (Luke 1:37).

However, the question to ask is, "Why did God take so long? Why as long as six days?" The answer is also given in Exodus 20:11, and that answer is the basis of the Fourth Commandment:

> For in six days the LORD made the heavens and the earth, the sea, and all that is in them, and rested the seventh day. Therefore the LORD blessed the Sabbath day and hallowed it.

The seven-day week has no basis outside of Scripture. In this Old Testament passage, God commands His people, Israel, to work for six days and rest for one—thus giving us a reason why He deliberately took as long as six days to create everything. He set the example for man. Our week is patterned after this principle. Now if He created everything in six thousand (or six million) years, followed by a rest of one thousand or one million years, then we would have a very interesting week indeed.

Some say that Exodus 20:11 is only an analogy in the sense that man is to work and rest—not that it was to mean six literal ordinary days followed by one literal ordinary day. However, Bible scholars have shown that this commandment "does not use analogy or archetypal thinking but that its emphasis is 'stated in terms of the imitation of God or a divine precedent that is to be followed.'"[20] In other words, it was to be six literal days of work, followed by one literal day of rest, just as God worked for six literal days and rested for one.

Some have argued that "the heavens and the earth" is just earth and perhaps the solar system, not the whole universe. However, this verse clearly says that God made *everything* in six days—six consecutive ordinary days, just like the commandment in the previous verse to work for six consecutive ordinary days.

The phrase "heaven(s) and earth" in Scripture is an example of a figure of speech called a *merism*, where two opposites are combined into an all-encompassing single concept, in this case the totality of creation. A linguistic analysis of the words "heaven(s) and earth" in Scripture shows that they refer to the totality of all creation (the Hebrews did not have a word for "universe"). For example, in Genesis 14:19 God is called "Creator of heaven and earth." In Jeremiah 23:24 God speaks of Himself as filling "heaven and earth." See also Genesis 14:22; 2 Kings 19:15; 2 Chronicles 2:12; Psalms 115:15, 121:2, 124:8, 134:3, 146:6; and Isaiah 37:16.

Thus, there is no scriptural warrant for restricting Exodus 20:11 to earth and its atmosphere or the solar system alone. So Exodus 20:11 does show that the whole universe was created in six ordinary days.

Implication

As the days of creation are ordinary days in length, then by adding up the years in Scripture (assuming no gaps in the genealogies[21]), the age of the universe is only about six thousand years.[22]

Refuting common objections to six literal days

Objection 1

"Science" has shown the earth and universe are billions of years old; therefore the "days" of creation must be long periods (or indefinite periods) of time.

Answer

1. The age of the earth, as determined by man's fallible methods, is based on unproven assumptions, so it is not proven that the earth is billions of years old.[23]

2. This unproven age is being used to force an interpretation on the language of the Bible. Thus, man's fallible theories are allowed to interpret the Bible. This ultimately undermines the use of language to communicate.

3. Evolutionary scientists claim the fossil layers over the earth's surface date back hundreds of millions of years. As soon as one allows millions of years for the fossil layers, then one has accepted death, bloodshed, disease, thorns, and suffering before Adam's sin.

The Bible makes it clear[24] that death, bloodshed, disease, thorns, and suffering are a *consequence* of sin.[25] In Genesis

1:29–30, God gave Adam and Eve and the animals plants to eat (this is reading Genesis at face value, as literal history, as Jesus did in Matthew 19:3–6). In fact, there is a theological distinction made between animals and plants. Human beings and higher animals are described in Genesis 1 as having a *nephesh*, or life principle. (This is true of at least the vertebrate land animals as well as the birds and fish: Genesis 1:20, 24.) Plants do not have this *nephesh*—they are not "alive" in the same sense animals are. They were given for food.

Man was permitted to eat meat only after the Flood (Genesis 9:3). This makes it obvious that the statements in Genesis 1:29–30 were meant to inform us that man and the animals were vegetarian to start with. Also, in Genesis 9:2, we are told of a change God apparently made in the way animals react to man.

God warned Adam in Genesis 2:17 that if he ate of the "tree of the knowledge of good and evil" he would "die." The Hebrew grammar actually means, "dying, you will die." In other words, it would be the commencement of a process of physical dying (see Genesis 3:19). It also clearly involved spiritual death (separation from God).

After Adam disobeyed God, the Lord clothed Adam and Eve with "coats of skins" (Genesis 3:21).[26] To do this He must have killed and shed the blood of at least one animal. The reason for this can be summed up by Hebrews 9:22:

> And according to the law almost all things are purified with blood, and without shedding of blood there is no remission.

God requires the shedding of blood for the remission of sins. What happened in the garden was a picture of what was to come in Jesus Christ, who shed His blood on the Cross as the Lamb of God who took away the sin of the world (John 1:29).

Now if the Garden of Eden were sitting on a fossil record of dead things millions of years old, then blood was shed before sin. This would destroy the foundation of the Atonement. The

PERFECT WORLD

RESTORATION

NEW HEAVEN
AND
NEW EARTH

INTRUSION
DEATH
DISEASE
PAIN
SUFFERING
EMOTIONAL
ANGUISH

Bible is clear: the sin of Adam brought death and suffering into the world. As Romans 8:19–22 tells us, the whole of creation "groans" because of the effects of the fall of Adam, and the creation will be liberated "from the bondage of corruption into the glorious liberty of the children of God" (Romans 8:21). Also, bear in mind that thorns came into existence after the Curse. Because there are thorns in the fossil record, it had to be formed after Adam and Eve sinned.

The pronouncement of the death penalty on Adam was both a curse and a blessing. A curse because death is horrible and continually reminds us of the ugliness of sin; a blessing because it meant the consequences of sin—separation from fellowship with God— need not be eternal. Death stopped Adam and his descendants from living in a state of sin, with all its consequences, forever. And because death was the just penalty for sin, Jesus Christ suffered physical death, shedding His blood, to release Adam's descendants from the consequences of sin. The Apostle Paul discusses this in depth in Romans 5 and 1 Corinthians 15.

Revelation 21–22 makes it clear that there will be a "new heavens and a new earth" one day, where there will be "no more death" and "no more curse"—just like it was before sin changed everything. If there are to be animals as part of the new earth, obviously they will not be dying or eating each other, nor eating the redeemed people!

Thus, adding the supposed millions of years to Scripture destroys the foundations of the message of the Cross.

Objection 2

According to Genesis 1, the sun was not created until Day 4. How could there be day and night (ordinary days) without the sun for the first three days?

Answer

1. Again, it is important for us to let the language of God's Word speak to us. If we come to Genesis 1 without any outside influences, as has been shown, each of the six days of creation appears with the Hebrew word *yom* qualified by a number and the phrase "evening and morning." The first three days are written the *same* way as the next three. So if we let the language speak to us, all six days were ordinary earth days.

2. The sun is not needed for day and night. What is needed is light and a rotating earth. On the first day of creation, God made light (Genesis 1:3). The phrase "evening and morning" certainly implies a rotating earth. Thus, if we have light from one direction, and a spinning earth, there can be day and night.

Where did the light come from? We are not told,[27] but Genesis 1:3 certainly indicates it was a created light to provide day and night until God made the sun on Day 4 to rule the day. Revelation 21:23 tells us that one day the sun will not be needed because the glory of God will light the heavenly city.

Perhaps one reason God did it this way was to illustrate that the sun did not have the priority in the creation that people have tended to give it. The sun did not give birth to the earth as evolutionary theories postulate; the sun was God's created tool to rule the day that God had made (Genesis 1:16).

Down through the ages, people such as the Egyptians have worshiped the sun. God warned the Israelites, in Deuteronomy 4:19, not to worship the sun as the pagan cultures around them did. They were commanded to worship the God who made the sun—not the sun that was *made* by God.

Evolutionary theories (the "big bang" hypothesis for instance) state that the sun came before the earth and that the sun's energy on the earth eventually gave rise to life. Just as in pagan beliefs, the sun is, in a sense, given credit for the wonder of creation.

It is interesting to contrast the speculations of modern cosmology with the writings of the early church father Theophilus:

> On the fourth day the luminaries came into existence. Since God has foreknowledge, he understood the nonsense of the foolish philosophers who were going to say that the things produced on Earth came from the stars, so that they might set God aside. In order therefore that the truth might be demonstrated, plants and seeds came into existence before stars. For what comes into existence later cannot cause what is prior to it.[28]

Objection 3

2 Peter 3:8 states that "one day is with the Lord as a thousand years," therefore the days of creation could be long periods of time.

Answer

1. This passage has *no* creation context—it is *not* referring to Genesis or the six days of creation.

2. This verse has what is called a "comparative article"—"as" or "like"—which is not found in Genesis 1. In other words, it is *not* saying a day *is* a thousand years; it is comparing a real, literal day to a real, literal thousand years. The context of this passage is the Second Coming of Christ. It is saying that, to God, a day is *like* a thousand years, because God is outside of time. God is not limited by natural processes and time as humans are. What may seem like a long time to us (e.g., waiting for the Second Coming), or a short time, is nothing to God, either way.

3. The second part of the verse reads "and a thousand years as one day," which, in essence, cancels out the first part of the verse for those who want to equate a day with a thousand years. Thus, it cannot be saying a day is a thousand years or vice versa.

4. Psalm 90:4 states, "For a thousand years in your sight are as yesterday when it is past, and as a watch in the night." Here a thousand years is being compared with a "watch in the night" (four hours[29]). Because the phrase "watch in the night" is joined in a particular way to "yesterday," it is saying that a thousand years is being compared with a short period of time—not simply to a day.

5. If one used this passage to claim that "day" in the Bible means a thousand years, then, to be consistent, one would have to say that Jonah was in the belly of the fish three thousand years, or that Jesus has not yet risen from the dead after two thousand years in the grave.

Objection 4

Insisting on six solar days for creation limits God, whereas allowing God billions of years does not limit Him.

Answer

Actually, insisting on six ordinary earth-rotation days of creation is not limiting *God*, but limiting *us* to believing that God actually did what He tells us in His Word. Also, if God created everything in six days, as the Bible says, then surely this reveals the power and wisdom of God in a profound way— Almighty God did not *need* eons of time. However, the billions-of-years scenarios diminish God by suggesting that mere chance could create things or that God needed huge amounts of time to create things—this would be limiting God's power by reducing it to naturalistic explanations.

Objection 5

Adam could not have accomplished all that the Bible states in one day (Day 6). He could not have named all the animals, for instance; there was not enough time.

Answer

Adam did not have to name *all* the animals—only those God brought to him. For instance, Adam was commanded to name "every beast of the field" (Genesis 2:20), not "beast of the earth" (Genesis 1:25). The phrase "beast of the field" is most likely a subset of the larger group "beast of the earth." He did not have to name "everything that creeps upon the earth" (Genesis 1:25) or any of the sea creatures.

Also, the number of "kinds" would be much less than the number of species in today's classification.

When critics say that Adam could not name the animals in less than one day, what they really mean is they do not understand how *they* could do it, so Adam could not. However, our brain has suffered from 6,000 years of the Curse—it has been greatly affected by the Fall. Before sin, Adam's brain was perfect.

When God made Adam, He must have programmed him with a perfect language. Today we program computers to "speak" and "remember." How much more could our Creator God have created Adam as a mature human (he was not born as a baby needing to learn to speak), having in his memory a perfect language with a perfect understanding of each word. (That is why Adam understood what God meant when he said he would "die" if he disobeyed, even though he had not seen any death.) Adam may also have had a "perfect" memory (something like a photographic memory, perhaps).

It would have been no problem for this first perfect man to make up words and name the animals God brought to him and remember the names—in far less than one day.[30]

Objection 6

Genesis 2 is a different account of creation, with a different order, so how can the first chapter be accepted as teaching six literal days?

Answer

Actually, Genesis 2 is not a *different* account of creation. It is a *more detailed* account of Day 6 of creation. Chapter 1 is an overview of the whole of creation; chapter 2 gives details surrounding the creation of the garden, the first man, and his activities on Day 6.[31] Between the creation of Adam and the creation of Eve, the King James Version says,

> "Out of the ground the Lord God formed every beast of the field and every fowl of the air" (Genesis 2:19).

This seems to say that the land beasts and birds were created between the creation of Adam and Eve. However, Jewish scholars did not recognize any such conflict with the account in chapter 1, where Adam and Eve were both created after the beasts and birds (Genesis 1:23–25). There is no contradiction, because in Hebrew the precise tense of a verb is determined by the context. It is clear from chapter 1 that the beasts and birds were created before Adam, so Jewish scholars would have understood the verb "formed" to mean "had formed" or "having formed" in Genesis 2:19 If we translate verse 19, "Now the Lord God had formed out of the ground all the beasts of the field," the apparent disagreement with Genesis 1 disappears completely.

Regarding the plants and herbs in Genesis 2:5 and the trees in Genesis 2:9 (compare with Genesis 1:12), the plants and herbs are described as "of the field" and they needed a man to tend them. These are clearly cultivated plants, not just plants in general (Genesis 1). Also, the trees (Genesis 2:9) are only the trees planted in the garden, not trees in general.

In Matthew 19:3–6 Jesus Christ quotes from both Genesis 1:27 and Genesis 2:24 when referring to the *same man and woman* in teaching the doctrine of marriage. Clearly, Jesus saw them as *complementary* accounts, *not* contradictory ones.

Objection 7

There is no "evening and morning" for the seventh day of the Creation Week (Genesis 2:2). Thus, we must still be in the "seventh day," so none of the days can be ordinary days.

Answer

Look again at the section entitled "Why Six Days?" above. Exodus 20:11 is clearly referring to seven literal days—six for work and one for rest.

Also, God stated that He "*rested*" from His work of creation (not that He *is resting!*). The fact that He rested from His work of creation does not preclude Him from continuing to rest from this activity. God's work now is different—it is a work of sustaining His creation and of reconciliation and redemption because of man's sin.

The word *yom* is qualified by a number (Genesis 2:2–3), so the context still determines that it is an ordinary solar day. Also, God blessed this seventh day and made it holy. In Genesis

3:17–19 we read of the Curse on the earth because of sin. Paul refers to this in Romans 8:22. It does not make sense that God would call this day holy and blessed if He cursed the ground on this "day." We live in a sin-cursed earth—we are not in the seventh blessed holy day!

Note that in arguing that the seventh day is not an ordinary day because it is not associated with "evening and morning," proponents are tacitly agreeing that the other six days are ordinary days because they are defined by an evening and a morning.

Some have argued that Hebrews 4:3–4 implies that the seventh day is continuing today:

> For we who have believed do enter that rest, as He has said: "So I swore in My wrath, 'They shall not enter My rest,'" although the works were finished from the foundation of the world. For He has spoken in a certain place of the seventh day in this way: "And God rested on the seventh day from all His works . . . ."

However, verse 4 reiterates that God rested (past tense) on the seventh day. If someone says on Monday that he rested on Friday and is still resting, this would not suggest that Friday continued through to Monday! Also, only those who have believed in Christ will enter that rest, showing that it is a spiritual rest, which is compared with God's rest since the Creation Week. It is not some sort of continuation of the seventh day (otherwise everyone would be "in" this rest).[32]

Hebrews does *not* say that the seventh day of Creation Week is continuing today, merely that the rest He instituted is continuing.

Objection 8

Genesis 2:4 states, "In the day that the Lord God made the earth and the heavens." As this refers to all six days of creation, it shows that the word "day" does not mean an ordinary day.

Answer

The Hebrew word *yom* as used here is *not* qualified by a number, the phrase "evening and morning," or light or darkness. In this context, the verse really means "in the time God created" (referring to the Creation Week) or "when God created."

Other problems with long days and similar interpretations

- If the plants made on Day 3 were separated by millions of years from the birds and nectar bats (created Day 5) and insects (created Day 6) necessary for their pollination, then such plants could not have survived. This problem would be especially acute for species with complex symbiotic relationships (each depending on the other; e.g., the yucca plant and the associated moth[33]).

- Adam was created on Day 6, lived through Day 7, and then died when he was 930 years old (Genesis 5:5). If each day were a thousand years or millions of years, this would make no sense of Adam's age at death.

- Some have claimed that the word for "made" (*asah*) in Exodus 20:11 actually means "show." They propose that God showed or revealed the information about creation to Moses during a six-day period. This allows for the creation itself to have occurred over millions of years. However, "showed" is not a valid translation for *asah*. Its meaning covers "to make, manufacture, produce, do," etc., but not "to show" in the sense of reveal.[34] Where *asah* is translated as "show"—for example, "show kindness" (Genesis 24:12)—it is in the sense of "to do" or "make" kindness.

- Some have claimed that because the word *asah* is used for the creation of the sun, moon, and stars on Day 4, and not the word *bara*, which is used in Genesis 1:1 for "create," this means God only revealed the sun, moon, and stars at this stage. They insist the word *asah* has the meaning of "revealed." In other words, the luminaries were supposedly already in existence and were only revealed at this stage. However, *bara* and *asah* are used in Scripture to describe the same event. For example, *asah* is used in Exodus 20:11 to refer to the creation of the heavens and the earth, but *bara* is used to refer to the creation of the heavens and the earth in Genesis 1:1. The word *asah* is used concerning the creation of the first people in Genesis 1:26—they did not previously exist. And then they are said to have been created (*bara*) in Genesis 1:27. There are many other similar examples. *asah* has a broad range of meanings involving "to do" or "to make," which includes *bara* creation.

- Some accept that the days of creation are ordinary days as far as the language of Genesis is concerned but not as literal days of history as far as man is concerned. This is basically the view called the "framework hypothesis."[35] This is a very complex and contrived view which has been thoroughly refuted by scholars.[36]

  The real purpose of the framework hypothesis can be seen in the following quote from an article by one of its proponents:

  > To rebut the literalist interpretation of the Genesis creation "week" propounded by the young-earth theorists is a central concern of this article.[37]

- Some people want the days of creation to be long periods in an attempt to harmonize evolution or billions of years with the Bible's account of origins. However, the order of events according to long-age beliefs does not agree with that of Genesis. Consider the following table:

**Contradictions between the order of creation
in the Bible and evolution/long-ages**

Biblical account of creation	Evolutionary/long-age speculation
Earth before the sun and stars	Stars and sun before earth
Earth covered in water initially	Earth a molten blob initially
Oceans first, then dry land	Dry land, then the oceans
Life first created on the land	Life started in the oceans
Plants created before the sun	Plants came long after the sun
Land animals created after birds	Land animals existed before birds
Whales before land animals	Land animals before whales

Clearly, those who do not accept the six literal days are the ones reading their own preconceived ideas into the passage.

Long-age compromises

Other than the "gap theory" (the belief that there is a gap of indeterminate time between the first two verses of Genesis 1), the major compromise positions that try to harmonize long ages and/or evolution with Genesis fall into two categories:

1. "Theistic evolution" wherein God supposedly directed the evolutionary process of millions of years, or even just set it up and let it run, and

2. "Progressive creation" where God supposedly intervened in the processes of death and struggle to create millions of species at various times over millions of years.

All long-age compromises reject Noah's Flood as global—it could only be a local event because the fossil layers are accepted as evidence for millions of years. A global Flood would have destroyed this record and produced another. Therefore, these positions cannot allow a catastrophic global Flood that would form layers of fossil-bearing rocks over the earth. This, of course, goes against Scripture, which obviously teaches a global Flood (Genesis 6–9).[38] Sadly, most theologians years ago simply tried to add this belief to the Bible instead of realizing that these layers were laid down by Noah's Flood.

Does it really matter?

Yes, it does matter what a Christian believes concerning the days of creation in Genesis 1. Most importantly, all schemes which insert eons of time into, or before, creation undermine the gospel by putting death, bloodshed, disease, thorns, and suffering before sin and the Fall, as explained above (see answer to Objection 1).

Here are two more reasons:

1. It is really a matter of how one approaches the Bible, in principle. If we do not allow the language to speak to us in context, but try to make the text fit ideas outside of Scripture, then ultimately the meaning of any word in any part of the Bible depends on man's interpretation, which can change according to whatever outside ideas are in vogue.

2. If one allows science (which has wrongly become synonymous with evolution and materialism) to determine our understanding of Scripture, then this can lead to a slippery slope of unbelief through the rest of Scripture. For instance, science would proclaim that a person cannot be raised from the dead. Does this mean we should interpret the Resurrection of Christ to reflect this? Sadly, some do just this, saying that the Resurrection simply means that Jesus' teachings live on in His followers.

When people accept at face value what Genesis is teaching and accept the days as ordinary days, they will have no problem accepting and making sense of the rest of the Bible.

Martin Luther once said:

I have often said that whoever would study Holy Scripture should be sure to see to it that he stays with the simple words as long as he can and by no means departs from them unless an article of faith compels him to understand them differently. For of this we must be certain: no clearer speech has been heard on Earth than what God has spoken.[39]

Pure words

God's people need to realize that the Word of God is something very special. It is not just the words of men. As Paul said in 1 Thessalonians 2:13, "You received it not as the word of men, but as it is, truly the word of God."

Proverbs 30:5–6 states that "every word of God is pure . . . . Do not add to His words, lest He reprove you and you be found a liar." The Bible cannot be treated as just some great literary work. We need to "tremble at his word" (Isaiah 6:5) and not forget:

> All Scripture is given by inspiration of God, and is profitable for doctrine, for reproof, for correction, for instruction in righteousness, that the man of God may be complete, thoroughly equipped for every good work (2 Timothy 3:16–17).

In the original autographs, every word and letter in the Bible is there because God put it there. Let us listen to God speaking to us through His Word and not arrogantly think we can tell God what He really means!

1. M. Van Bebber and P. Taylor, "Creation and Time: A Report on the Progressive Creationist Book by Hugh Ross, Films for Christ," Mesa, Arizona, 1994.

2. G. Hasel, The "days" of creation in Genesis 1: literal "days" or figurative "periods/epochs" of time? Origins 21(1):5–38, 1994.

3. Martin Luther as cited in E. Plass, What Martin Luther Says: A Practical In-Home Anthology for the Active Christian, Concordia Publishing House, St. Louis, Missouri, 1991, 1523.

4. G. Archer, A Survey of Old Testament Introduction, Moody Press, Chicago, 1994, 196–197.

5. J. Boice, *Genesis: An Expositional Commentary, Vol. 1, Genesis 1:1–11*, Zondervan Publishing House, Grand Rapids, 1982, 68.

6. C.H. Spurgeon, *The Sword and the Trowel*, 1877, 197.

7. L. Berkhof, *Introductory volume to Systematic Theology*, Wm. B. Eerdmans, Grand Rapids, Michigan, 1946, 60, 96.

8. F. Brown, S. Driver, and C. Briggs, *A Hebrew and English Lexicon of the Old Testament*, Clarendon Press, Oxford, 1951, 398.

9. Some say that Hosea 6:2 is an exception to this because of the figurative language. However, the Hebrew idiomatic expression used, "After two days . . . in the third day," meaning "in a short time," makes sense only if "day" is understood in its normal sense.

10. J. Stambaugh, "The days of creation: a semantic approach," *TJ* 5(1):70–78, April 1991. Available online at www.answersingenesis.org/go/days; Editor's note: there is a slightly updated version of this paper published later at the Evangelical Theological Society that made the case even stronger.

11. The Jews start their day in the evening (sundown followed by night), obviously based on the fact that Genesis begins the day with the "evening."

12. Stambaugh, The days of creation: a semantic approach, 75.

13. Ibid., 72.

14. Ibid., 72–73.

15. Ibid., 72–73; R. Grigg, "How long were the days of Genesis 1?" *Creation* 19(1):23–25, 1996.

16. J. Barr, personal letter to David Watson, April 23, 1984.

17. M. Dods, *Expositor's Bible*, T & T Clark, Edinburgh, 1888, 4, as cited by D. Kelly, *Creation and Change*, Christian Focus Publications, Fearn, Scotland, 1997, 112.

18. Plass, *What Martin Luther Says: A Practical In-Home Anthology for the Active Christian*, 1523.

19. J. McNeil, Ed., *Calvin: Institutes of the Christian Religion 1*, Westminster Press, Louisville, Kentucky, 1960, 160–161, 182.

20. G. Hasel, "The 'days' of creation in Genesis 1: literal 'days' or figurative 'periods/epochs' of time?" *Origins* 21(1):29, 1994.

21. J. Whitcomb and H. Morris, *The Genesis Flood*, Presbyterian and Reformed Publ., Phillipsburg, New Jersey, 1961, 481–483, Appendix II. They allow for the possibility of gaps in the genealogies because the word "begat" can skip generations. However, they point out that even allowing for gaps would give a maximum age of around 10,000 years.

22. L. Pierce, "The forgotten archbishop," *Creation* 20(2):42–43, 1998. Ussher carried out a very scholarly work in adding up all the years in Scripture to obtain a date of creation of 4004 BC. Ussher has been mocked for stating that creation occurred on October 23—he obtained this date by working backward using the Jewish civil year and accounting for how the year and month were derived over the years. Thus, he didn't just pull this date out of the air but gave a scholarly mathematical basis for it. This is not to say this is the correct date, as there are assumptions involved, but the point is, his work is not to be scoffed at. Ussher did not specify the hour of the day for creation, as some skeptics assert. Young's Analytical Concordance, under "creation," lists many other authorities, including extrabiblical ones, who all give a date for creation of less than 10,000 years ago.

23. H. Morris and J. Morris, *Science, Scripture, and the Young Earth*, Institute for Creation Research, El Cajon, California, 1989, 39–44; J. Morris, *The Young Earth*, Master Books, Green Forest, Arkansas, 1996, 51–67; S. Austin, *Grand Canyon: Monument to Catastrophe*, Institute for Creation Research, El Cajon, California, pp. 1994, 111–131; L. Vardiman, ed., *Radio Isotopes and the Age of the Earth*, Vol. 2, Master Books, Green Forest, Arkansas, 2005.

24. K. Ham, *The Lie: Evolution*, Master Books, Green Forest, Arkansas, Introduction, 1987, xiii–xiv; K. Ham, "The necessity for believing in six literal days," *Creation* 18(1):38–41, 1996; K. Ham, "The wrong way round!" *Creation* 18(3):38–41, 1996; K. Ham, "Fathers, promises and vegemite," *Creation* 19(1):14–17, 1997; K. Ham, "The narrow road," *Creation* 19(2):47–49, 1997; K. Ham, "Millions of years and the 'doctrine of Balaam,'" *Creation* 19(3):15–17, 1997.

25. J. Gill, *A Body of Doctrinal and Practical Divinity*, 1760. Republished by Primitive Baptist Library, Carthage, Illinois, 1980, 191. This is not just a new idea from modern scholars. In 1760 John Gill, in his commentaries, insisted there was no death, bloodshed, disease, or suffering before sin.

26. All Eve's progeny, except the God-man Jesus Christ, were born with original sin (Romans 5:12, 18–19), so Eve could not have conceived when she was sinless. So the Fall must have occurred fairly quickly, before Eve had conceived any children (they were told to "be fruitful and multiply").

27. Some people ask why God did not tell us the source of this light. However, if God told us everything, we would have so many books we would not have time to read them. God has given us all the information we need to come to the right conclusions about the things that really matter.

28. L. Lavallee, "The early church defended creation science," *Impact*, No. 160, p. ii, 1986. Quotation from Theophilus "To Autolycus," 2.8, Oxford Early Christian Texts.

29. The Jews had three watches during the night (sunset to 10 pm; 10 pm to 2 am; 2 am to sunrise), but the Romans had four watches, beginning at 6 pm.

30. R. Grigg, "Naming the animals: all in a day's work for Adam," *Creation* 18(4):46–49, 1996.

31. D. Batten, "Genesis contradictions?" *Creation* 18(4):44–45, 1996; M. Kruger, "An understanding of Genesis 2:5," *CEN Technical Journal* 11(1):106–110, 1997.

32. Anon., "Is the Seventh Day an eternal day?" *Creation* 21(3):44–45, 1999.

33. F. Meldau, *Why We Believe in Creation Not in Evolution*, Christian Victory Publ., Denver, Colorado, 1972, 114–116.

34. Nothing in Gesenius's Lexicon supports the interpretation of asah as "show"; See Charles Taylor's "Days of Revelation or creation?" (1997) found at www.answersingenesis.org/docs/188.asp.

35. M. Kline, "Because it had not rained," *Westminster Theological Journal* 20:146–157, 1957–1958.

36. Kruger, *An understanding of Genesis 2:5*, 106–110; J. Pipa, "From chaos to cosmos: a critique of the framework hypothesis," presented at the Far-Western Regional Annual Meeting of the Evangelical Theological Society, USA, April 26, 1996; Wayne Grudem's *Systematic Theology*, InterVarsity Press, Downers Grove, Illinois, 1994, 302–305, summarizes the framework hypothesis and its problems and inconsistencies.

37. M. Kline, "Space and time in the Genesis cosmology," *Perspectives on Science & Christian Faith* 48(1), 1996.

38. M. Van Bebber and P. Taylor, *Creation and Time: A Report on the Progressive Creationist Book by Hugh Ross*, 55–59; Whitcomb and Morris, *The Genesis Flood*, 212–330.

39. Plass, *What Martin Luther Says: A Practical In-Home Anthology for the Active Christian*, 93.

From the Beginning of . . . the Institution of Marriage?

Terry Mortenson

Respected Christian apologists Dr. John Ankerberg[1] and Dr. Norman Geisler[2] have launched another attack on young-earth creationism (YEC), this time by objecting in a web article to the frequent YEC use of Mark 10:6, from which we argue that Jesus was a young-earth creationist and so we should be too, if we call Him our Lord.

Ironically in a little 1991 booklet on evolution,[3] Ankerberg and co-author John Weldon mention Matthew 19:4–5 (the parallel passage to Mark 10:6) as part of their defense of the young-earth view. They even state that they have studied the various old-earth reinterpretations of Genesis "in detail and believe they all have fatal biblical flaws." It is tragic that Ankerberg has since ignored Jesus' teaching and his own reasoning based on it (or perhaps they were Weldon's arguments and Ankerberg only helped write other parts of the booklet).

In any case, it is clear from Ankerberg's comments when moderating the Hovind-Ross debate (with an unfair old-earth bias) that he picked up many compromise views at his seminary. And as shown by Dr. David Menton's letter to Ankerberg in June 1992, Ankerberg was clearly an old-earther at about the time of the booklet. This letter shows the disrespectful way Ankerberg treated high-profile young-earth creationist PhD scientists, who had given up much time to record programs for him, and instead he substituted the gross errors of old-earther Hugh Ross.

But consider now Ankerberg's and Geisler's current handling of Mark 10:6 in their web article. In response to a question from the Pharisees about divorce Jesus replied in that verse, "But from the beginning of creation, God made them male and female."

In their article, "Differing Views of the 'Days' of Creation," Ankerberg and Geisler (A/G) first state the YEC reasoning on Mark 10:6 and then give their objections to that view.

VIII. Mark 10:6 Affirms That Adam and Eve Were Created at the Beginning

Argument: According to this text, "At the beginning of creation God 'made them male and female.'" If God created humankind at the beginning of Creation, then they were not created at the end of millions of years, as the old-earth view contends.

Response: First, Adam was not created at the beginning but at the end of the creation period (on the sixth day), no matter how long or short the days were. Second, the Greek word for "create" (*ktisis*) can and sometimes does mean "institution" or "ordinance" (cf. 1 Peter 2:13). Since Jesus is speaking of the institution of marriage in Mark 10:6, it could mean "from the beginning of the institution of marriage." Third, and finally, even if Mark 10:6 is speaking of the original creation events, it does not mean there could not have been a long period of time involved in those creative events.

Below I first restate their argument point by point, which is indented, and then offer my refutation of each point.

A/G response 1: First, Adam was not created at the beginning but at the end of the creation period (on the sixth day), no matter how long or short the days were.

Notice that they have slipped in the word "period." But Jesus didn't say Adam and Eve were created at the beginning of the "creation period" (i.e., the beginning of Creation Week). He said at the "beginning of creation." He is talking about the whole creation from Jesus' day back to the very first moment of creation, just as Paul is referring to the whole creation during all of history in Romans 1:18–20 and Romans 8:19–23. In other words, Jesus is saying that Adam and Eve were created at the beginning of history.

This is seen also in the parallel passage to Mark 10:6 found in Matthew 19:4, where Jesus says that Adam and Eve were simply "at the beginning." Jesus uses the exact same Greek words (translated as "from the beginning of the creation") in Mark 13:19 and in the verse is clearly speaking of all time from the first day of creation to His day. Compare also His reference to the similar phrase "from the foundation of the world" in Luke 11:50–51. By adding one word ("period"), Ankerberg and Geisler have put a certain spin on what their Lord said and therefore misinterpreted Him. So, this objection to the YEC argument from this verse fails.

A/G response 2: Second, the Greek word for "create" (*ktisis*) can and sometimes does mean "institution" or "ordinance" (cf. 1 Peter 2:13). Since Jesus is speaking of the institution of marriage in Mark 10:6, it could mean "from the beginning of the institution of marriage."

They argue that *ktisis* (which is actually the noun "creation" not the verb "create," as A/G say) in Mark 10:6 should be translated as "institution" so that Jesus should be understood to be talking about the beginning of the institution of marriage, not the beginning of creation. They base this interpretation on the fact that in 1 Pet 2:13 *ktisis* is translated in the NIV as "to every authority instituted among men" or in the NASB as "to every human institution." But they have not paid careful attention to the presence of "among men" (NIV) and "human" (NASB) in this verse.

The Greek text is clear. The phrase under question is *pasē anthrōpinē ktisei*, where the whole phrase is in the dative case (so literally "to every human creation") and the adjective *anthrōpinē* ("human") modifies *ktisei* ("creation"). An institutional authority

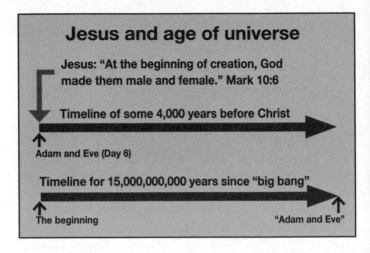

Jesus and age of universe

Jesus: "At the beginning of creation, God made them male and female." Mark 10:6

Timeline of some 4,000 years before Christ

↑ Adam and Eve (Day 6)

Timeline for 15,000,000,000 years since "big bang"

↑ The beginning

↑ "Adam and Eve"

(such as kings, governors, and slave masters, which Peter discusses in the context) is indeed a "human creation." But this is a very different contextual use of *ktisis* than we find in Mark 10:6, where no adjective is used to modify "creation." Furthermore, in Mark 10:6 Jesus could have easily said "from the first marriage" or "from the beginning of marriage" or "since God created man" or "since God created Adam," if that is what He meant.

Finally, if we give *ktisis* in Mark 10:6 the meaning "authority" or "institution," it makes no sense. What does from the beginning of authority or beginning of institution mean? To make it meaningful Ankerberg and Geisler would have to add a word to the text, which would have no contextual justification.

Jesus is reaching farther back in history for the basis of his teaching on marriage. The Pharisees go back to the time of Moses' writings in Deuteronomy, whereas Jesus goes back to the beginning of time. Jesus spoke these words about 4000 years after the beginning. If we equate those 4000 years with a 24-hour day, then Jesus was speaking at 24:00 and the creation of Adam and Eve on the sixth literal day of history would be equivalent to 00:00:00:35

(half a second after the beginning), in the non-technical language of Jesus here is the beginning of time. So, Jesus is indeed saying that Adam and Eve were at the beginning of creation.

A/G response 3: Third, and finally, even if Mark 10:6 is speaking of the original creation events, it does not mean there could not have been a long period of time involved in those creative events.

This is very odd reasoning from two men who usually display such excellent logic in their writings and speaking. If Jesus is saying that Adam and Eve were at the beginning of creation, as He clearly was, then it should be patently obvious that there can be no long period of time (billions of years are what Ankerberg and Geisler want to fit in to Genesis 1) before Adam and Eve. If the universe is truly about 15 billion years old as the evolutionists insist (and these two Christian leaders accept) and if the first true man and woman evolved into existence only about 100–200 thousand years ago (as evolutionists contend, or if Adam and Eve were supernaturally created only a few tens of thousands of years ago, as Ankerberg and Geisler probably believe) then Adam and Eve would not be at the "beginning of creation" but at the tail end of the creation to-date! If true, Jesus could hardly be more mistaken.

So Mark 10:6 (along with other statements of Jesus in the Gospels) clearly shows that Jesus took Genesis as literal history and was a young-earth creationist.[4] And since Drs. Ankerberg and Geisler call Him "Lord" they should repent of their old-earth teachings and join YECs in calling the church back to the authority of the Word of God beginning from the very first verse, so that with greater credibility the church can proclaim the gospel and the moral standards of Scripture to a rebellious and lost "evolutionized" world.

The rest of the Ankerberg/Geisler article could be similarly refuted, but that would make this article too long. Most of their arguments (which are not unique to them) are handled by Chaffey and Lisle in *Old Earth Creationism on Trial*.[5] Though it is primarily a thorough and insightful exposé of the many serious errors in the teachings of Hugh Ross, which both Ankerberg and Geisler have endorsed, it also refutes other old-earth arguments. And to see that the idea of millions of years (which is clearly driving Ankerberg's and Geisler's reinterpretations of Mark 10:6 and Genesis) did not come from the rocks and fossils but from anti-biblical philosophical/religious presuppositions applied to the rocks and fossils, see my book, *The Great Turning Point*.[6] These two books are must-reading for every seminary professor, pastor and other Christian leaders.

---

1.   Ankerberg is the producer and host of the influential Christian TV program, "The John Ankerberg Show." He has also written many helpful books.

2.   Geisler is a prominent philosopher, former president of the Evangelical Theological Society, current president of Southern Evangelical Seminary and author of an amazing number of useful books.

3.   See John Ankerberg and John Weldon, *The Facts on Creation vs. Evolution*, Harvest House, Eugene, OR, p. 43, 1991.

4.   Mortenson, T., "Jesus, evangelical scholars, and the age of the earth," Answers in Depth, August 1, 2007, http://www.answersingenesis.org/articles/aid/v2/n1/jesus-and-the-age-of-earth.

5.   Chaffey, T., and Lisle, J., *Old Earth Creationism on Trial*, Master Books, Green Forest, AR, 2008.

6.   Mortenson, T., *The Great Turning Point*, Master Books, Green Forest, AR, 2004.

Terry Mortenson earned his doctorate in history of geology from England's University of Coventry and his MDiv from Trinity Evangelical Divinity School in Deerfield, Illinois. He is a popular writer, speaker, and researcher for Answers in Genesis–USA.

Why Did God Take Six Days?

Ken Ham

When people accept at face value what Genesis is teaching and accept the days as ordinary days, they will have no problem understanding what the rest of Genesis is all about.

When one picks up a Bible, reads Genesis chapter 1, and takes it at face value, it seems to say that God created the world, the universe, and everything in them in six ordinary (approximately 24 hour) days. However, there is a view in our churches which has become prevalent over the years that these "days" could have been thousands, millions, or even billions of years in duration. Does it really matter what length these days were? Is it possible to determine whether or not they were ordinary days, or long periods of time?

What is a "day?"

The word for "day" in Genesis 1 is the Hebrew word *yom*. It can mean either a day (in the ordinary 24-hour day), the daylight portion of an ordinary 24-hour day (i.e., day as distinct from the night), or occasionally it is used in the sense of an indefinite period of time (e.g., "in the time of the Judges" or "In the day of the Lord"). Without exception, in the Hebrew Old Testament the word *yom* never means "period" (i.e., it is never used to refer to a definite long period of time with specific beginning and end points). The word which means a long period of time in Hebrew is *olam*. Furthermore, it is important to note that even when the word yom is used in the indefinite sense, it is clearly indicated by the context that the literal meaning of the word "day" is not intended.

Some people say the word "day" in Genesis may have been used symbolically and is thus not meant to be taken literally.

However, an important point that many fail to consider is that a word can never be symbolic the first time it is used! In fact, a word can only be used symbolically when it has first had a literal meaning. In the New Testament we are told that Jesus is the "door." We know what this means because we know the word "door" means an entrance. Because we understand its literal meaning, it is able to be applied in a symbolic sense to Jesus Christ, so we understand that "He" is not literally a door. The word "door" could not be used in this manner unless it first had the literal meaning we understand it to have. Thus, the word "day" cannot be used symbolically the first time it is used in the Book of Genesis, as this is where God not only introduced the word "day" into the narrative, but also defined it as He invented it. Indeed, this is why the author of Genesis has gone to great lengths to carefully define the word "day" the first time it appears. In Genesis 1:4 we read, "And God saw the light, that it was good; and God divided the light from the darkness" called "night." Genesis 1:5 then finishes with: "And God called the light Day, and the darkness he called Night. And the evening and the morning were the first day." This is the same phrase used for each of the other five days and shows there was a clearly established cycle of days and nights (i.e., periods of light and periods of darkness).

A day and the sun

But how could there be day and night if the sun wasn't in existence? After all, it is clear from Genesis 1 that the sun was not created until day four. Genesis 1:3 tells us that God created light on the first day, and the phrase "evening and morning" shows there were alternating periods of light and darkness. Therefore, light was in existence, coming from one direction upon a rotating earth, resulting in the day and night cycle. However, we are told exactly where this light came from. The word for "light" in Genesis 1:3 means the substance of light that was created. Then, on day four in Genesis 1:14–19 we are told of the creation of the sun which was to be the source of light from that time onward. The sun was created to rule the day that already existed. The day stayed the same. It merely had a new light source. The first three days of creation (before the sun) were the same type of days as the three days with the sun. Perhaps God deliberately left the creation of the sun until the fourth day because He knew that down through the ages cultures would try to worship the sun as the source of life. Not only this, modern theories tell us the sun came before the earth. God is showing us that He made the earth and light to start with, that He can sustain it with its day and night cycle and that the sun was created on Day Four as a tool of His to be the bearer of light from that time.

Probably one of the major reasons people tend not to take the days of Genesis as ordinary days is because they believe that scientists have proved the earth to be billions of years old. But this is not true. There is no absolute age-dating method to determine how old the earth is. Besides this, there is much evidence consistent with a belief in a young age for the earth, perhaps only thousands of years.

Incidentally, those who say that a day could be millions of years must answer the question, "What is a night?"

Why six days?

God is an infinite being. He has infinite power, infinite knowledge, infinite wisdom. Obviously, God could then make anything He desired. He could have created the whole universe, the earth and all it contains in no time at all. Perhaps the question we should be asking is why did God take as long as six days? After all, six days is a peculiar period for an infinite being to make anything. The answer can be found in Exodus 20:11. Exodus 20 contains the Ten Commandments, and it should be remembered that these commandments were written on stone by the very "finger of God." In Exodus we read:

"And he gave unto Moses, when he had made an end of communing with him upon mount Sinai, two tables of testimony, tables of stone, written with the finger of God" (Exodus 31:18). The fourth commandment, in verse 9 of chapter 20, tells us that we are to work for six days and rest for one. The justification for this is given in verse 11: "For in six days the Lord made heaven and earth, the sea, and all that in them is, and rested the seventh day; wherefore the Lord blessed the sabbath day, and hallowed it." This is a direct reference to God's Creation Week in Genesis 1. To be consistent (and we must be), whatever is used as the meaning of the word "day" in Genesis 1 must also be used here. If you are going to say the word "day" means a long period of time in Genesis, then it has been already shown that the only way this can be is in the sense of the "day" being an indefinite or indeterminate period of time, not a definite period of time. Thus, the sense of Exodus 20:9–11 would have to be "six indefinite periods shalt thou labor and rest a seventh indefinite period." This, however, makes no sense at all. By accepting the days as ordinary days, we understand that God is telling us He worked for six ordinary days and rested one ordinary day to set a pattern for man—the pattern of our seven-day week which we still have today.

Day-age inconsistencies

There are many inconsistencies in accepting the days in Genesis as long periods of time. For instance, we are told in Genesis 1:26–28 that God made the first man (Adam) on the sixth day. Adam lived through the rest of the sixth day and through the seventh day. We are told in Genesis 5:5 that he died when he was 930 years old. (We are not still in the seventh day as some people misconstrue, for Genesis 2:2 tells us God "rested" from His work of creation, not that He is resting from His work of creation.) If each day was, for example, a million years, then there are real problems. In fact, if each day were only a thousand years long, this still makes no sense of Adam's age at death either.

A day is as a thousand years

But some then refer to 2 Peter 3:8 which tells us: "But, beloved, be not ignorant of this one thing, that one day is with the Lord as a thousand years, and a thousand years as one day." This verse is used by many who teach, by inference at least, that the days in Genesis must each be a thousand years long. This reasoning, however, is quite wrong. Turning to Psalm 90:4 we read a similar verse: "For a thousand years in thy sight are but as yesterday when it is past, and as a watch in the night." In both 2 Peter (3) and Psalm 90 the whole context is that God is neither limited by natural processes nor by time. To the contrary, God is "outside" time, for He also "created" time. Neither verse refers to the days of creation in Genesis, for they are dealing with God not being bound by time. In 2 Peter 3, the context is in relation to Christ's Second Coming, pointing out the fact that with God a day is just like a thousand years or a thousand years is just like one day. He is outside of time. This has nothing to do with the days of creation in Genesis.

Further, in 2 Peter 3:8 the word "day" is contrasted with "a thousand years." The word "day" thus has a literal meaning which enables it to be contrasted with "a thousand years." It could not be contrasted with "a thousand years" if it didn't have a literal meaning. Thus, the thrust of the Apostle's message is that God can do in a very short time what men or "nature" would require a very long time to accomplish, if they could accomplish it at all. It is interesting to note that evolutionists try to make out that the chance, random processes of "nature" required millions of years to produce man. Many Christians have accepted these millions of years, added them to the Bible and then said that God took millions of years to make everything. However, the point of 2 Peter 3:8 is that God is not limited by time, whereas evolution requires time (a very great deal of it!).

Days and years

In Genesis 1:14 we read that God said, "Let there be lights in the firmament of the heaven to divide the day from the night; and let them be for signs, and for seasons, and for days, and years." If the word "day" here is not a literal day, then the word "years" being used in the same verse would be meaningless.

Day and covenant

Turning to Jeremiah 33:25–26 we read: "Thus saith the Lord; If my covenant be not with day and night, and if I have not appointed the ordinances of heaven and earth; then will I cast away the seed of Jacob, and David my servant so that I will not take any of his seed to be rulers over the seed of Abraham, Isaac, and Jacob; for I will cause their captivity to return, and have mercy on them." The Lord is telling Jeremiah that He has a covenant with the day and the night which cannot be broken, and it is related to the promise to the descendants of David, including the One who was promised to take the throne (Christ). This covenant between God and the day and night began in Genesis 1, for God first defined and invented day and night when He spoke them into existence.

There is no clear origin for day and night in the Scripture other than Genesis 1. Therefore, this must be the beginning of this covenant. So if this covenant between the day and the night does not exist when God clearly says it does (i.e., if you do not take Genesis 1 to literally mean six ordinary days), then this promise given here through Jeremiah is on shaky ground.

Does the length of the day matter?

Finally, does it really matter whether we accept them as ordinary days or not? The answer is a most definite "Yes!" It is really a principle of how one approaches the Bible. For instance, if we don't accept them as ordinary days then we have to ask the question,

"What are they?" The answer is "We don't know." If we approach the days in this manner, then to be consistent we should approach other passages of Genesis in the same way. For instance, when it says God took dust and made Adam—what does this mean? If it does not mean what is says, then we don't know what it means! We should take Genesis literally. Furthermore, it should be noted that you cannot "interpret literally," for a "literal interpretation" is a contradiction in terms. You either take it literally or you interpret it! It is important to realize we should take it literally unless it is obviously symbolic, and when it is symbolic either the context will make it quite clear or we will be told in the text.

If a person says that we do not know what the word "day" means in Genesis, can another person who says they are literal days be accused of being wrong? The answer is "No," because the person who accepts them as ordinary days does know what they mean. It is the person who does not know what the days mean who cannot accuse anyone of being wrong.

People try to make the word "day" say something else be cause they are trying to make room for the long ages of evolutionary geology. This doesn't work because these supposed ages are repre-sented by fossils showing death and struggle, and thus you are left with the same old problem of death and struggle before Adam. The Bible clearly indicates that there was no death and suffering before Adam's sin.

When people accept at face value what Genesis is teaching and accept the days as ordinary days, they will have no problem understanding what the rest of Genesis is all about.

"For in six days the Lord made heaven and earth, the sea,
and all that in them is, and rested the seventh day; wherefore the
Lord blessed the sabbath day, and hallowed it" (Exodus 20:11).

Did Bible Authors Believe in a Literal Genesis?

Terry Mortenson

Anyone who has read the Bible very much will recognize that there are different kinds of literature in the Old and New Testaments. There are parables, poetry, prophetic visions, dreams, epistles, proverbs, and historical narrative, with the majority being the latter. So, how should we interpret Genesis 1–11? Is it history? Is it mythology? Is it symbolic poetry? Is it allegory? Is it a parable? Is it a prophetic vision? Is it a mixture of these kinds of literature or some kind of unique genre? And does it really matter anyway?

We will come back to the last question later, but suffice it to say here that the correct conclusion on genre of literature is foundational to the question of the correct interpretation. If we interpret something literally which the author intended to be understood figuratively, then we will misunderstand the text. When Jesus said "I am the door" (John 10:9), He did not mean that He was made of wood with hinges attached to His side. Conversely, if we interpret something figuratively that the author intended to be taken literally, we will err. When Jesus said, "The Son of Man is about to be betrayed into the hands of men, and they will kill Him, and the third day He will be raised up" (Matthew 17:22–23), He clearly meant it just as literally as if I said to my wife, "Margie, I'm going to fill up the gas tank with gas and will be back in a few minutes."

There are many lines of evidence we could consider to determine the genre of Genesis 1–11, such as the internal evidence within the book of Genesis and how the church has viewed these chapters throughout church history. But in this chapter we want to answer the question, "How did the other biblical authors

Moses as depicted in the Creation Museum's biblical authority room.

(besides Moses, who wrote Genesis[1]) and Jesus interpret them?" From my reading and experience it appears that most people who consider the question of how to interpret the early chapters of Genesis have never asked, much less answered, that question.

To begin, consider what God says about the way He spoke to Moses in contrast to the way He spoke to other prophets. In Numbers 12:6–8 we read:

Then He said, "Hear now My words: if there is a prophet among you, I, the LORD, make Myself known to him in a vision; I speak to him in a dream. Not so with My servant Moses; he is faithful in all My house. I speak with him face to face, even plainly, and not in dark sayings; And he sees the form of the LORD. Why then were you not afraid to speak against My servant Moses?"

So, God says that He spoke "plainly" to Moses, not in "dark sayings," that is, not in obscure language. That strongly suggests that we should not be looking for mysterious, hard-to-understand meanings in what Moses wrote. Rather, we should read Genesis as the straightforward history that it appears to be. An examination of how the rest of the Bible interprets Genesis confirms this.

Old Testament authors and their use of Genesis

When we turn to other Old Testament authors, there are only a few references to Genesis 1–11. But they all treat those chapters as literal history.

The Jews were very careful about genealogies. For example, in

Nehemiah 7:61–64 the people who wanted to serve in the rebuilt temple needed to prove that they were descended from the priestly line of Aaron. Those who could not prove this could not serve as priests. 1 Chronicles 1–8 gives a long series of genealogies all the way back to Adam. Chapter 1 (verses 1–28) has no missing or added names in the genealogical links from Adam to Abraham, compared to Genesis 5 and 11. The author(s) of 1 Chronicles obviously took these genealogies as historically accurate.

Outside of Genesis 6–11, Psalm 29:10 contains the only other use of the Hebrew word *mabbul* (translated "flood").[2] God literally sat as King at the global Flood of Noah. If that event was not historical, the statement in this verse would have no real force and the promise of verse 11 will give little comfort to God's people.

Psalm 33:6–9 affirms that God created supernaturally by His Word, just as Genesis 1 says repeatedly. Creatures came into existence instantly when God said, "Let there be . . ." God did not have to wait for millions or thousands of years for light or dry land or plants and animals or Adam to appear. "He spoke and it was done; He commanded and it stood fast" (Psalm 33:9).

Psalm 104:5 and 19 speak of events during Creation Week.[3] But verses 6–9 in this psalm give additional information to that provided in Genesis 8, which describes how the waters receded off the earth at the end of the Flood.[4] The psalmist is clearly describing historical events.

In beautiful poetic form, Psalm 136 recounts many of God's mighty acts in history, beginning with statements about some of His creative works in Genesis 1.

David, the writer of many of the psalms, from a Creation Museum display.

Isaiah recorded God's Words, not mythical tales.

In Isaiah 54:9 God says (echoing the promise of Psalm 104:9) to Israel, "For this is like the waters of Noah to Me; for as I have sworn that the waters of Noah would no longer cover the earth, so have I sworn that I would not be angry with you, nor rebuke you." The promise of God would have no force, if the account of Noah's Flood was not historically true. No one would believe in the Second Coming of Christ if the promise of it was given as, "Just as Santa Claus comes from the North Pole in his sleigh pulled by reindeer on Christmas Eve and puts presents for the whole family under the Christmas tree in each home, so Jesus is coming again as the King of Kings and Lord of Lords." In fact, the analogy would convince people that the Second Coming is a myth.

In Ezekiel 14:14–20 God refers repeatedly to Noah, Daniel, and Job and clearly indicates that they were all equally historical and righteous men. There is no reason to doubt that God meant that everything the Bible says about these men is historically accurate.

New Testament authors' view of Genesis

The New Testament has many more explicit references to the early chapters of Genesis.

The genealogies of Jesus presented in Matthew 1:1–17 and Luke 3:23–38 show that Genesis 1–11 is historical narrative. These genealogies must all be equally historical or else we must conclude that Jesus was descended from a myth and therefore He would not have been a real human being and therefore not our Savior and Lord.[5]

Paul built his doctrine of sin and salvation on the fact that sin and death entered the world through Adam. Jesus, as the Last Adam, came into the world to bring righteousness and life to people and to undo the damaging work of the first Adam (Romans 5:12–19; 1 Corinthians 15:21–22, 15:45–47.). Paul affirmed that the serpent deceived Eve, not Adam (2 Corinthians 11:3; 1 Timothy 2:13–14). He took Genesis 1–2 literally by affirm-

Paul relied heavily on a Genesis as plainly written.

ing that Adam was created first and Eve was made from the body of Adam (1 Corinthians 11:8–9). In Romans 1:20 Paul indicated that people have seen the evidence of God's existence and some of His attributes since the creation of the world.[6] That means that Paul believed that man was right there at the beginning of history, not billions of years after the beginning.

Peter similarly based some of his teachings on the literal history of Genesis 1–11. In 1 Peter 3:20; 2 Peter 2:4–9, 3:3–7, he referred to the Flood. He considered the account of Noah and the Flood just as historical as the account of the judgment of Sodom and Gomorrah (Genesis 19). He affirmed that only eight people were saved and that the Flood was global, just as the future judgment at the Second Coming of Christ will be. He argued that scoffers will deny the Second Coming because they deny the supernatural Creation and Noah's Flood. And Peter told his readers that scoffers will do this because they are reasoning on the basis of the philosophical assumption which today we call uniformitarian naturalism: "all things continue as they were from the beginning of creation" (2 Peter 3:4).[7]

The words of John and Peter demonstrate their trust in the historicity of the Genesis accounts.

It has been objected that the apostles did not know the difference between truth and myth. But this is also false. In 1 Corinthians 10:1–11 Paul refers to a number of passages from the Pentateuch where miracles are described and he emphasizes in verses 6 and 11 that "these things happened." In 2 Timothy 4:3–4 Paul wrote:

> For the time will come when they will not endure sound doctrine, but according to their own desires, because they have itching ears, they will heap up for themselves teachers; and they will turn their ears away from the truth, and be turned aside to fables.

The Greek word translated here as "fables" is *muthos*, from which we get our English word "myth." In contrast to "truth" or "sound doctrine," the same Greek word is used in 1 Timothy 1:4, 4:7; Titus 1:14; and 2 Peter 1:16. In a first-century world filled with Greek, Roman, and Jewish myths, the apostles clearly knew the difference between truth and myth. And they constantly affirmed that the Word of God contains truth, not myth.

Christ and His use of Genesis

In John 10:34–35 Jesus defended His claim to deity by quoting from Psalm 82:6 and then asserting that "Scripture cannot be broken." That is, the Bible is faithful, reliable, and truthful. The Scriptures cannot be contradicted or confounded. In Luke 24:25–27 Jesus rebuked His disciples for not believing all that the prophets have spoken (which He equates with "all the Scriptures"). So, in Jesus's view, all Scripture is trustworthy and should be believed.

Another way that Jesus revealed His complete trust in the Scriptures was by treating as historical fact the accounts in the Old Testament, which most contemporary people think are unbelievable mythology. These historical accounts include Adam and Eve as the first married couple (Matthew 19:3–6; Mark 10:3–9), Abel as the first prophet who was martyred (Luke 11:50–51), Noah and the Flood (Matthew 24:38–39), the experiences of Lot and his wife (Luke 17:28–32), the judgment of Sodom and Gomorrah (Matthew 10:15), Moses and the serpent in the wilderness wanderings after the exodus from Egypt (John 3:14), Moses and the manna from heaven (John 6:32–33, 6:49), the miracles of Elijah (Luke 4:25–27), and Jonah in the big fish (Matthew 12:40–41).

As Wenham has compellingly argued,[8] Jesus did not allegorize these accounts but took them as straightforward history, describing events that actually happened, just as the Old Testament describes. Jesus used these accounts to teach His disciples that the events of His own death, resurrection, and second coming would likewise certainly happen in time-space reality. Jesus indicated that the Scriptures are essentially perspicuous (or clear): eleven times the gospel writers record Him saying, "Have you not read . . .?"[9] And thirty times He defended His teaching by saying "It is written."[10] He rebuked His listeners for not understanding and believing what the text plainly says.

Besides the above-mentioned evidence that Jesus took Genesis 1–11 as straightforward reliable history, the Gospel writers record three important statements that reveal Jesus's worldview. Careful analysis of these verses (Mark 10:6, 13:19–20; Luke 11:50–51) shows that Jesus believed that Adam and Eve were in existence essentially at the same time that God created everything else (and Abel was very close to that time), not millions or billions of years after God made the other things.[11] This shows that Jesus took the creation days as literal 24-hour days. So, everything Jesus said shows that we can justifiably call Him a young-earth creationist.

It has been objected that in these statements Jesus was just accommodating the cultural beliefs of His day. But this is false for four reasons. First, Jesus was the truth (John 14:6), and therefore He always spoke the truth. No deceitful or misleading words ever came from His mouth (1 Peter 2:22). Even his enemies said, "Teacher, we know that you are truthful, and defer to no one; for you are not partial to any, but teach the way of God in truth" (Mark 12:14). Second, Jesus taught with authority on the basis of God's Word, which He called "truth" (John 17:17), not as the scribes and Pharisees taught based on their traditions (Matthew 7:28–29).

Third, Jesus repeatedly and boldly confronted all kinds of wrong thinking and behavior in His listeners' lives, in spite of the threat of persecution for doing so (Matthew 22:29; John 2:15–16, 3:10, 4:3–4, 4:9; Mark 7:9–13). And finally, Jesus emphasized the foundational importance of believing what Moses wrote in a straight-forward way (John 5:45; Luke 16:31, 24:25–27, 24:44–45; John 3:12; Matthew 17:5).

Why is this important?

We should take Genesis 1–11 as straightforward, accurate, literal history because Jesus, the apostles, and all the other biblical writers did so. There is absolutely no biblical basis for taking these chapters as any kind of non-literal, figurative genre of literature. That should be reason enough for us to interpret Genesis 1–11 in the same literal way. But there are some other important reasons to do so.

Only a literal, historical approach to Genesis 1–11 gives a proper foundation for the gospel and the future hope of the gospel. Jesus came into the world to solve the problem of sin that started in real, time-space history in the real Garden of Eden with two real people called Adam and Eve and a real serpent that spoke to Eve.[12] The sin of Adam and Eve resulted in spiritual and physical death for them, but also a divine curse on the once "very good" all of creation (see Genesis 1:31 and 3:14–19). Jesus is coming again to liberate all Christians and the creation itself from that bondage to corruption (Romans 8:18–25). Then there will be a new heaven and a new earth, where righteousness dwells and where sin, death, and natural evils will be no more. A non-literal reading of Genesis destroys this message of the Bible and ultimately is an assault on the character of God.[13]

Genesis is also foundational to many other important doctrines in the rest of the Bible, such as male loving headship in the home and the church.

Conclusion

The Bible is crystal clear. We must believe Genesis 1–11 as literal history because Jesus, the New Testament apostles, and the Old Testament prophets did, and because these opening chapters of Genesis are foundational to the rest of the Bible.

As we and many other creationists have always said, a person doesn't have to believe that Genesis 1–11 is literally true to be saved. We are saved when we repent of our sins and trust solely in the death and resurrection of Jesus Christ for our salvation (John 3:16; Romans 10:9–10). But if we trust in Christ and yet disbelieve Genesis 1–11, we are being inconsistent and are not faithful followers of our Lord.

God said through the prophet Isaiah (66:1–2):

> Thus says the LORD: "Heaven is My throne, and earth is My footstool. Where is the house that you will build Me? And where is the place of My rest? For all those things My hand has made, and all those things exist, says the LORD. But on this one will I look: on him who is poor and of a contrite spirit, and who trembles at My word."

Will you be one who trembles at the words of God, rather than believing the fallible and erroneous words of evolutionists who develop hypotheses and myths that deny God's Word? Ultimately, this question of the proper interpretation of Genesis 1–11 is a question of the authority of God's Word.

---

1. That Moses was the author of the first five books (called the Pentateuch) of the Old Testament is clear from Scripture itself. The Pentateuch explicitly claims this in Exodus 17:14, 24:4, 34:27; Numbers 33:1–2; Deuteronomy 31:9–11. Other OT books affirm that Moses wrote these books which by the time of Joshua became known collectively as "the Law," "the book of the Law," or "the Law of Moses": Joshua 1:8, 8:31–32; 1 Kings 2:3; 2 Kings 14:6 (quoting Deuteronomy 24:16), 21:8; Ezra 6:18; Nehemiah 13:1; Daniel 9:11–13; Malachi 4:4. The New Testament agrees in Matthew 19:8; John 5:46–47, 7:19; Acts 3:22 (quoting from Deuteronomy 18:15); Romans 10:5 (quoting from Leviticus 18:5), and Mark 12:26 (referring to Exodus 3:6). Jewish tradition also ascribes the Pentateuch to Moses. Also, the theories of liberal theologians who deny the Mosaic authorship of these books are fraught with false assumptions and illogical reasoning. See Gleason L. Archer, Jr., *A Survey of Old Testament Introduction* (Chicago: Moody Press, 1985), pp. 109–113.

2. There are four other Hebrew words that are used in the OT to describe lesser, localized floods.

3. Most of this psalm is referring to aspects of God's creation as it existed at the time the psalmist was writing. Contrary to what some old-earth creationists assert, Psalm 104 is not a "creation account."

4. That these verses do not refer to Creation Week is evident from the promise reflected in verse 9, which echoes the promise of Genesis 9:11–17. God made no such promise on the third day of Creation Week when He made dry land appear.

5. In Matthew 1:1–17, Matthew has clearly left out some names in his genealogy (for a literary purpose), as seen by comparing it to the Old Testament history, but all the names are equally historical all the way back to Abraham, who is first mentioned in Genesis 11. Luke 3:23–38 traces the lineage of Jesus back to Adam. There is no reason to think there are any missing names in Luke's genealogy, because 1) he was concerned about giving us the exact truth (Luke 1:4) and 2) his genealogy from Adam to Abraham matches 1 Chron. 1:1–28 and Genesis 5 and 11, and there is no good reason for concluding that Genesis has missing names. See Ken Ham and Larry Pierce, "Who Begat Whom? Closing the Gap in Genesis Genealogies," www.answersingenesis.org/articles/am/v1/n2/who-begat-whom, and Travis R. Freeman, "Do the Genesis 5 and 11 Genealogies Contain Gaps?" in Terry

---

Mortenson and Thane H. Ury, eds., *Coming to Grips with Genesis* (Green Forest, AR: Master Books, 2008), pp. 283–314.

6. The New King James and the King James Version translate the Greek in this verse as "from the creation of the world." The word "from" in English has a similar range of meanings as the Greek word (*apo*) that it translates here. There are a number of reasons to take it in a temporal sense, meaning "since" as the NAS, NIV, and ESV translate it. For a fuller discussion of this important verse, see Ron Minton, "Apostolic Witness to Genesis Creation and the Flood," in Terry Mortenson and Thane H. Ury, eds., *Coming to Grips with Genesis* (Green Forest, AR: Master Books, 2008), pp. 351–354.

7. For more discussion of this see Terry Mortenson, "Philosophical Naturalism and the Age of the Earth: Are They Related?" *The Master's Seminary Journal* 15 no. 1 (2004): 71–92, online at www.answersingenesis.org/docs2004/naturalismChurch.asp.

8. John Wenham, *Christ and the Bible* (Downers Grove, IL: InterVarsity Press, 1973), pp. 11–37.

9. In these instances Jesus referred to Genesis 1–2, Exodus 3–6, 1 Samuel 21:6, Psalm 8:2, Psalm 118:22, and to unspecified Levitical law—in other words, to passages from the historical narrative, the Law, and the poetry of Scripture.

10. Passages He specifically cited were from all five books of the Pentateuch, Psalms, Isaiah, Jeremiah, Zechariah, and Malachi. Interestingly, in the temptation of Jesus, Satan used Scripture literally and, in response, Jesus did not imply that the literal interpretation of Satan was wrong. Rather He corrected Satan's misapplication of the text's literal meaning by quoting another text, which He took literally (see Matthew 4:6–7).

11. See Terry Mortenson, "Jesus' View of the Age of the Earth," in Terry Mortenson and Thane H. Ury, eds., *Coming to Grips with Genesis* (Green Forest, AR: Master Books, 2008), pp. 315–346.

12. Why Christians have trouble believing Genesis 3 when it speaks of a talking serpent is a mystery to me. We have talking parrots today, which involves no miracles. And if the Christian believes in any miracles of the Bible, then he must believe that Balaam's donkey was used by God to speak to the false prophet (Numbers 22:28). Since Satan is a supernatural being who can do supernatural things (e.g., 2 Corinthians 11:11–13; Matthew 4:1–11; 2 Thessalonians 2:8–9), it is not difficult at all to understand or believe that he could speak through a serpent to deceive Eve (cf. 2 Corinthians 11:3; Revelation 12:9).

13. See Ken Ham and James Stambaugh, "Whence Cometh Death? A Biblical Theology of Physical Death and Natural Evil," and Thane H. Ury, "Luther, Calvin, and Wesley on the Genesis of Natural Evil: Recovering Lost Rubrics for Defending a Very Good Creation," in Terry Mortenson and Thane H. Ury, eds., *Coming to Grips with Genesis* (Green Forest, AR: Master Books, 2008), pp. 373–398 and 399–424, respectively.

Eisegesis: A Genesis Virus

Ken Ham

A deadly virus is sweeping through church members worldwide. Investigators have found that the reason this virus is fairly specific to church attendees is that it has found safe harbour in many seminaries and Bible colleges.

In these institutions, the virus is transmitted to students who eventually pass it on to unsuspecting church members (especially if they become pastors). Although some people are "immune" to the effects of the virus, most are not. The virus has been called "The Eisegesis Virus," and has been found responsible for the "death" of many church members.

This report summarizes the nature of this "virus" that does not affect a person's physical body, but infects their thinking in such a way that people are no longer able to consistently determine absolute truth. I consider this virus to be one of the most dangerous in the world today.

There is, however, a powerful vaccine that can counteract the eisegesis "virus" and even reverse its destructive effects on thinking. The vaccine, called "exegesis," is readily available, but sadly is not recognized by most church leaders.

Now I am not referring to a biological virus or a physical vaccine, but to what I could call a "spiritual virus"—a way of thinking that has taken over the minds of many church leaders and most church members. This has caused them to incorrectly interpret God's holy Word. This often results in doubt about, or even unbelief in, biblical doctrines. It has placed a stumbling block before people in the world, one which results in them scoffing at, and not being willing to take seriously, the words of Scripture.

The antidote is a "spiritual vaccine" that teaches a way to think that enables people to "interpret" God's Word correctly and believe and understand this special revelation of absolute truth. As a result, people in the world are challenged, and many hearts are changed in regard to their attitude towards God's Word and the gospel of Jesus Christ.

The eisegesis "virus"

The Random House *Webster's Unabridged Dictionary* defines "eisegesis" as: "an interpretation, esp. of Scripture, that expresses the interpreter's own ideas, bias, or the like, rather than the meaning of the text."

Thus, when someone reads something into Scripture—this would be an example of eisegesis. For instance, nowhere does the Bible ever speak of billions of years. In Genesis 1, the word day (*yom*) in context, as used for the six Days of Creation (with a number and the phrase evening and morning), means these days are approximately 24-hour periods—ordinary days.

EISEGESIS
'Reading into'

Genesis 1

3Then God said, "Let there be light"; and there was light. 4And God saw the light, that it was good; and God divided the light from the darkness. 5God called the light Day, and the darkness He called Night. So the evening and the morning were the first day.

YÔM really means "long age"

Millions of years

eisegesis (n., pl.) eis·e·ge·sis

1. an interpretation, esp. of Scripture, that expresses the interpreter's own ideas, bias, or the like, rather than the meaning of the text.

The Random House Webster's Unabridged Dictionary

However, probably the majority of church leaders insist these days could represent billions of years—this is "eisegesis", as the billions of years is a belief from outside of Scripture that is read into Scripture (resulting in the clear words of Scripture being reinterpreted on the basis of these outside ideas).

Sadly, this is the "virus" that infects much of the church. Church leaders and thus church members have, by and large, developed a way of thinking that accepts many aspects of what the "world" teaches concerning billions of years, evolution etc., and that reads these ideas into God's Word.

The "world" then views the church as not believing God's Word as written, but as accepting the "world's" theories as truth and reinterpreting God's Word to fit. Thus, the "world" does not really have a respect for the Bible and generally does not listen to the message of the Gospel that is preached from this book.

Many church members (and particularly their children and subsequent generations) recognize that if the Bible has to be reinterpreted on the basis of the "world's" teachings, then the Bible is not absolute truth. When they are taught to use eisegesis in Genesis, they begin to consistently apply this same interpretation method to the rest of the Bible. Ultimately, they stop taking the Bible seriously, and within a generation or two, people begin to reject the Christian faith and stop attending church. Thus, we see the "death" of many church members.

However, there is a powerful solution to this situation that can result in saving faith for many, and restoration of confidence for God's people in God's Word.

The exegesis "vaccine"

The Random House *Webster's Unabridged Dictionary* defines "exegesis" as: "critical explanation or interpretation of a text or portion of a text, esp. of the Bible."

Genesis 1

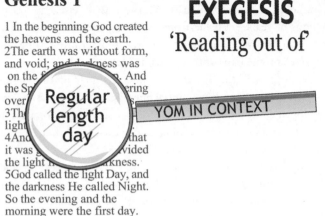

1 In the beginning God created the heavens and the earth.
2 The earth was without form, and void; and darkness was on the face of the deep. And the Spirit of God was hovering over the face of the waters.
3 Then God said, "Let there be light"; and there was light.
4 And God saw the light, that it was good; and God divided the light from the darkness.
5 God called the light Day, and the darkness He called Night. So the evening and the morning were the first day.

EXEGESIS
'Reading out of'

YOM IN CONTEXT

This is often called the "grammatical-historical" interpretation method.

Thus, when someone reads the words of Scripture, and interprets them on the basis of context and the type of literature etc., then this would be an example of "exegesis"—reading out of Scripture what the writer clearly intended to express.

In Genesis 1, the Hebrew word for day (*yom*), as used for each of the six Days of Creation, would be looked at in regard to context and the type of literature. Genesis is written in typical Hebrew historical narrative—this is important to understand when interpreting the words of this book. Any reputable Hebrew lexicon (one-way dictionary) will list the different meanings given to a word (like "day"), and the various contexts that determine these meanings.

One will find that whenever *yom* (day) is qualified by a number or the phrase evening and morning, it always means an ordinary day. Thus, critically looking at the text and then reading out of Scripture, one cannot come to any other conclusion except that these days were ordinary (24-hour) days.

When church members and their subsequent generations are trained in this method of thinking (interpreting Scripture in context), they have a respect for God's Word and then judge the "world's" fallible theories on the basis of what the Word of God clearly states. When they are taught to use exegesis in Genesis, they usually consistently apply this method of interpretation throughout the rest of the Bible. They have a solid faith in absolute truth. Especially when they then see how, starting with the history given in the Bible, they can make better sense of the same evidence which was previously used to undermine the Bible. They are not tossed "to and fro" by the world's fallible ideas, but by and large stand firm on the authoritative Word.

The "world" then recognizes that Christians do take God's Word seriously and believe it as written. As a result, the "world" is often challenged to question its fallible theories and listen to God's Word—instead of the other way around.

Understanding the difference between "eisegesis" and "exegesis" is really the key to the effectiveness of the church in today's culture.

Which "key" are you using?

All of this can be summed up by using the analogy of keys. These two interpretative methods are really two different keys:

These two keys unlock doors—each of which results in very different consequences when opened. The doors represent words—in this case, the words from the Bible. To illustrate the result of using these different keys, the two doors will represent the Hebrew word for day, *yom*.

The "exegesis key" unlocks door #1

This method of interpretation involves making God's Word the authority and letting its words speak to us—reading out of Scripture. Thus, starting with Genesis, one would take the words

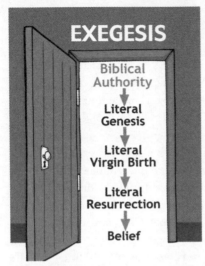

EXEGESIS

Biblical
Authority

↓

Literal
Genesis

↓

Literal
Virgin Birth

↓

Literal
Resurrection

↓

Belief

of this book as written. *Yom* in this context would be taken as exactly what it was meant to convey—an ordinary day.

If one consistently applies this same method of interpretation throughout the Scriptures, one would have no problem accepting the Virginal Conception and the literal bodily Resurrection of Christ. Such teachings come only from the revelation of Scripture—the words of the Bible taken in context according to the type of literature. This results in believing the words of Scripture, not doubting them, thus providing the basis for the Christian faith.

The "eisegesis key" unlocks door #2

This method of interpretation involves taking man's word (ideas, theories, etc.) from outside the Bible as a basis for reading into Scripture. Thus, starting with Genesis, one would take the words of this book (like the word day—*yom*) and interpret them in the light of man's fallible theories (e.g., billions of years). Even though the words taken as written in context contradict those outside ideas, their meaning must be changed to conform to them. This results in people doubting the Word of God, as it means one can't trust the words as written.

If a person then applies this interpretive method consistently throughout Scripture, one would certainly doubt the rest of Genesis (for example, the "world" teaches there never was a global

Flood), and ultimately other crucial doctrines (science has never shown a virgin birth in humans, for instance), including the bodily Resurrection of Christ (science has never shown that a man can be raised from the dead). This leads, consistently and logically, to disbelieving the words of Scripture, and thus rejecting the Christian faith that is built on the Bible.

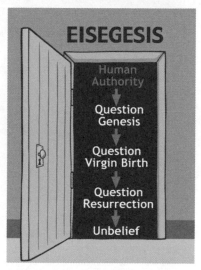

Sadly, the church is infected with the eisegesis "virus"—and as a result, the Christian worldview that was once so prevalent in the Western world is waning.

God's people need a good dose of the exegesis "vaccine" to restore the foundations of God's Word that the Christian worldview is built upon.

As Martin Luther said:

> I have often said that whoever would study Holy Scripture should be sure to see to it that he stays with the simple words as long as he can and by no means departs from them unless an article of faith compels him to understand them differently. For of this we must be certain: no simpler speech has been heard on Earth than what God has spoken.[1]

---

1.   Compiled by Plass, E.M., *What Martin Luther Says—A Practical In-Home Anthology for the Active*, Concordia Publishing House, St Louis, USA, p. 93, 1959.

Is the Age of the Earth a Salvation Issue?

Ken Ham and Bodie Hodge

Can a person believe in world that is millions and billions of years old and be a Christian? First of all, let's consider a few verses that summarize an understanding of the gospel and salvation.

> Moreover, brethren, I declare to you the gospel which I preached to you, which also you received and in which you stand, by which also you are saved, if you hold fast that word which I preached to you—unless you believed in vain.

> For I delivered to you first of all that which I also received: that Christ died for our sins according to the Scriptures, and that He was buried, and that He rose again the third day according to the Scriptures. (1 Corinthians 15:1–4)

> And if Christ is not risen, your faith is futile; you are still in your sins! (1 Corinthians 15:17)

> . . . if you confess with your mouth the Lord Jesus and believe in your heart that God has raised Him from the dead, you will be saved. (Romans 10:9)

> Jesus answered and said to him, "Most assuredly, I say to you, unless one is born again, he cannot see the kingdom of God." (John 3:3)

Of course, we could cite numerous other passages, but not one of them states in any way that one has to believe in a young earth/universe to be saved. And when one considers the list of those who "will not inherit the kingdom of God" (1 Corinthians 6:9–10), we certainly do not see "old earthers" listed in such passages.

Many great men of God who are now with the Lord have believed in an old earth. Some of these explained the millions of years by adopting the classic Gap Theory. Others accepted a Day-Age Theory or positions such as Theistic Evolution, the Framework Hypothesis, or Progressive Creationism.

Undoubtedly, Scripture plainly teaches salvation is conditioned upon faith in Christ, with no requirement for what one believes about the age of the earth/universe. In light of this, some people assume then that for a Christian, it does not matter what one believes concerning the age of the earth and universe. However, even though it is not a salvation issue, a Christian who believes in millions of years reaps severe consequences.

The issue of authority

The belief in millions of years does not come *from* Scripture, but from the secularist fallible dating methods used to date the age of the earth and universe. To even attempt to fit millions of years into the Bible, one has to invent a gap of time that is not allowed by the text or reinterpret the days of creation (that are obviously ordinary-length days in the context of Genesis 1) as long periods of time.

In other words, one has to add something (millions of years) from outside the Scripture into the Word of God. This is putting man's fallible ideas *in authority* over the Word of God. Thus one unlocks a door to do this in other areas. It is opening a door that others can push open further and further—which is what tends to happen with each successive generation. Once the door of compromise is open, even just a little, subsequent generations push the door open wider. Ultimately, this is a major contributing factor to the loss of biblical authority in our Western world.

> Do not add to His words, lest He rebuke you, and you be found a liar. (Proverbs 30:6)

The issue of contradiction

In many instances the belief in millions of years totally contradicts the clear teaching of Scripture. Here are just three:

1. Thorns – Fossil thorns are found in the fossil record, supposedly hundreds of millions of years old. So these supposedly existed millions of years before man. However, the Bible makes it clear that thorns only came into existence *after* the curse:

> Then to Adam He said, "Because you have . . . eaten from the tree of which I commanded you, saying, 'You shall not eat of it': Cursed is the ground for your sake . . . Both thorns and thistles it shall bring forth for you." (Genesis 3:17–18)

2. Disease – Evidence of diseases like cancer, brain tumors, and arthritis can be found in the fossil remains of animals said to be millions of year old. So these diseases supposedly existed millions of years before sin. The Scripture teaches us that after God finished creating everything, with man as the pinnacle of creation, He described the creation as "*very good*" (Genesis 1:31, emphasis added). Certainly, God calling cancer and brain tumors "very good" does not fit with the nature of God as described in Scripture.

3. Diet – Genesis 1:29–30 explain that Adam and Eve and all the animals were vegetarian before sin entered the world. However, the fossil record includes many examples of animals eating other animals—supposedly millions of years before man and thus before sin.

The issue of death

Romans 8:22 reveals that the whole creation groans because of the consequences of the Fall—the entrance of sin. One of the reasons it groans is because of death—death of living creatures, both animals and man. Death is described as an "enemy" (1 Corinthians 15:26), and one day death will be thrown into the lake of fire (Revelation 20:14). Romans 5:12 and other passages declare that physical death of man (and really, death in general) entered the once perfect creation because of man's sin. However, if one believes in millions of years, then there were millions of years of death, disease, suffering, carnivorous activity, and thorns before sin.

The first death was in the Garden of Eden when God killed an animal as the first blood sacrifice (Genesis 3:21)—a picture of what was to come in Jesus Christ, the Lamb of God, who would take away the sin of the world.

Jesus Christ stepped into history and paid the penalty required by our sin—death—by dying on the Cross. He conquered death when He rose from the dead. Although holding to an old earth is not a salvation issue per se, we believe that when a Christian insists on millions of years of death before sin it is really an attack on the work of Christ on the Cross.

> "And God will wipe away every tear from their eyes; there shall be no more death, nor sorrow, nor crying. There shall be no more pain, for the former things have passed away." (Revelation 21:4)

In a culture where the foundation of the gospel has come under attack by the concept of millions of years, it makes sense why the next generation is walking away from the church. Believing in millions of years may not affect *that person's* salvation, but it can affect the next generation—particularly in their witness. It is simply a matter of putting two and two together: if the foundation of the gospel (i.e., Genesis 1–11) is not true, then why would the gospel be true? Kids in the next generation can put *and have been* putting this together (see Ken Ham's book co-authored with Britt Beemer called *Already Gone.*)

If people believe the opening chapters of the Bible, then why can't they trust the rest? Conversely, if people do not believe the opening chapters of the Bible, when do they think God starts to tell the truth in His Word? We, as Christians, need to start teaching the Bible—including Genesis—as the authority in every area of our lives.

When witnessing to a culture influenced by millions of years, we have found it tremendously effective to explain the "Genesis Ground" of the "Romans Road." That is, we explain the foundation of the gospel found in Genesis before explaining the gospel message of Christ's sacrificial and atoning death, and subsequent burial, and Resurrection. In this way we counter the evolutionary ideas that have infiltrated the minds of the next generation. We teach the bad news in Genesis, and then we proclaim the "good news" (the gospel) that is rooted and grounded in the bad news. We call this the "Genesis-Romans Road" approach.

Genesis—Romans Road

Genesis 1:1 – God made everything.

"In the beginning God created the heavens and the earth."

Genesis 1:31 – God made everything perfectly—no death or suffering.

"Then God saw everything that He had made, and indeed it was very good. So the evening and the morning were the sixth day."

Genesis 3:17–19 – The punishment for sin is death; due to sin, the world is no longer perfect.

"Then to Adam He said, 'Because you have heeded the voice of your wife, and have eaten from the tree of which I commanded you, saying, "You shall not eat of it": Cursed is the ground for your sake; in toil you shall eat of it all the days of your life. Both thorns and thistles it shall bring forth for you, and you shall eat the herb of the field. In the sweat of your face you shall eat bread till you return to the ground, for out of it you were taken; for dust you are, and to dust you shall return.'"

Romans 5:12 – Because our mutual grandfather Adam sinned, we now sin too.

"Therefore, just as through one man sin entered the world, and death through sin, and thus death spread to all men, because all sinned."

Romans 3:23 – We need to realize we are all sinners, including ourselves.

"For all have sinned and fall short of the glory of God."

Romans 6:23 – The punishment for sin is a just punishment—death—but God came to rescue us and give the free gift of salvation by sending His Son, Jesus.

"For the wages of sin is death, but the gift of God is eternal life in Christ Jesus our Lord."

Romans 10:9 – You need to believe in Jesus; salvation is not by works, but by faith (see also John 3:16 and Acts 16:30–31).

"that if you confess with your mouth the Lord Jesus and believe in your heart that God has raised Him from the dead, you will be saved."

Romans 5:1 – Being saved, you are now justified and have peace with God.

"Therefore, having been justified by faith, we have peace with God through our Lord Jesus Christ."